F

SORROWS

TO

SAPPHIRES

*FREEDOM FROM THE SHAME
OF CHILD SEXUAL ABUSE*

ANGELA
WILLIAMS

MW00511301

ADVISORY: This does NOT contain graphic or sexually explicit material. It DOES contain the actual language used by Angela's abuser. Some readers may find this language offensive by some readers.
Parental guidance is strongly recommended.

© 2008, 2009, 2011, 2013 ANGELA K. WILLIAMS.

ALL RIGHTS RESERVED, ALL FORMS OF MEDIA INCLUDING BUT NOT LIMITED TO DIGITAL, ELECTRONIC, MOTION PICTURE AND TELEVISION SCRIPTS, BOOKS, WEBSITES, BROCHURES, SPEECHES, EDUCATIONAL INFORMATION, DOCUMENTARIES, AND TRAINING PROGRAMS, FOR BOTH PROFIT AND NON-PROFIT USES. ALL INTERNATIONAL RIGHTS RESERVED.

ANY USE OF THE TITLE OR ORIGINAL CONTENTS HEREIN WITHOUT WRITTEN PERMISSION IS PROHIBITED, EXCEPT FOR REVIEWERS WHO USE NO MORE THAN 100 WORDS IN REVIEWS FOR PUBLICATION AND REGISTER THEIR USE WITH THE COPYRIGHT HOLDER. FURTHER PERMISSION TO USE: CONTACT 678.644.5589 AND WWW.ANGELAKWILLIAMS.COM, ANGELA@ANGELAKWILLIAMS.COM .

Art Direction:
Shan Wallace

Concept & Cover Design:
SDW DESIGN :: ATLANTA, GA :: 678 446 1273
shan@gamads.com

Library of Congress Cataloging-in-Publication Data
1 – Biography; 2 – American Families; 3 – Incest; 4 - Child Sexual Abuse
FROM SORRORS TO SAPPHIRES – INCEST, SILENCE AND GOD
Angela K. Williams, Marietta, Georgia, USA

ISBN 0-978-1-939800-0
Fourth Printing 2013

DEDICATION

To my family – my husband Phil, my daughter Ashley, my son Jacob – whose love and support have been my oxygen.

Paula –
I pray my words
touch your heart
with hope and healing
Love!

Isaiah
54:11

3

4

FOREWORD

What a privilege it is for me to offer this opening to a true and powerful book. I write with joy and pride in a remarkable woman who has let our Lord use her brokenness to remold the clay of her life. It describes what I believe in my heart is truly a "treasure in an earthen vessel." I have seen Him working in her for more than 20 years. I have walked with her on the path of pain from her past, I have personally witnessed her broken heart, I have been there every time she heard God telling her to write this book and to take this as her ministry, revealing with living proof how God can take awful sorrows and turn them into awesome sapphires. I thank God every day for bringing this woman into my life and for blessing our love and our union as husband and wife.

Our love for one another, which is so strong and endures on so many levels, is only a small glimpse of the depth of love that God has for us all. I believe you will be both enraged and encouraged as you see her move from the depths of miry evil to the heights of delivery and reaffirmation by a great and good God. From the very first prayer she offered for a "happy family," to praying for healing and release of pain and guilt, to praying over issues of forgiveness, to prayers of affirmation and protection in putting this in print, we prayed that He would lead and guide and provide the opportunities and resources to make this book a reality. We prayed for a cathartic release from past pain for her, but more importantly for others who have and are suffering from child-abuse wounds – all to the glory of God alone.

To me, and to those who know Angela and the way she lives, her life is already a best-seller. Hers is a real-life revelation of how the free will that God grants us may also place us in life situations that have lasting effects on people's lives. It shows how bad things happen but can be used in a powerful and meaningful ways by God. It shows how a cold and hardhearted person, devoid of God, impacts daily lives, but this story also reveals how a loving and caring God can bring a victim out of pain and suffering to heal and restore him or her to a beautiful and precious jewel. With God's grace and power, He can truly turn sorrows into sapphires. I am witness to this love and restoration, and I claim this as one of the cornerstones for my faith and my walk with Christ.

Her dream, which I share, is to ignite a passion for the exposure of a silent epidemic and give voice to those who live with their own deadly secret. She has offered many valuable resources including specific help for a child in danger (see Chapter 23). I pray for those who read this book who have suffered through similar memories, the nightmares, and anguish. My prayer is that this book and its testimony may touch you and encourage you. *I Love You*, Angela, and I thank God for bringing you into my life and for you bringing me into a closer walk with Him.

–Phillip Williams
Marietta, Ga.

TABLE OF CONTENTS

CHAPTER 1

Silence Hides Abusers

O you afflicted, storm
tossed and not
comforted, behold, I
will set your stones in
fair colors, and lay
your foundations with
sapphires.
– Isaiah 54:11

I sit reading the headline: "Incest Out of Control." I feel the sting of the words that swirl in my mind: "Please Daddy, please, please stop!" The report says, "Because so few survivors are willing to speak up, there is a tragically small database emerging in the United States about the evil of incest. A lone statistic is telling enough: *One out of every six victims of rape in the U.S. is likely to be under the age of 12!* That projects to more than 20,000 annually – or about six young lives shattered every single day of the year! Horror among horrors is that 1 in 5 children under 12 who are incestuously assaulted are victims of their fathers - natural or by marriage or adoption.[1] And who has documented the number of suicides attributable to incest?"

"Add one who tried," I mutter and read on:

- Experts say 1 in 4 girls and 1 in 6 boys are sexually abused before their 18th birthdays.
- 1 in 5 children are sexually solicited on the Internet.
- The median age for reported sexual abuse is 9!

- Approximately 20% of the victims of sexual abuse are under age 8.
- 50% of all victims of forcible sodomy, sexual assault with an object, and forcible fondling are under 12.
- Nearly 40% are abused by older or larger children.
- 70-80% of sexual abuse survivors report excessive drug and alcohol use.
- One study showed that among male survivors, 50% have suicidal thoughts and more than 20% attempt suicide. [2]

My heart races as I identify with every single data point. If it is so widespread, why isn't more done about it? I know I am not alone, yet few speak of the evil done to us as children. Our voice is muted. The story continues:

The data is fiendishly flawed because so-called experts say that interviews with child survivors cannot be "reliably" reported. This official repression of information aids those who assault children! I am far from the first to complain of this official neglect. Former U.S. Senator Paula Hawkins of Florida held Senate hearings on the "disbelief and denial" problem two decades ago, documenting that children *can* be accurate in their telling of their abuse. Senator Hawkins herself disclosed at that time her own account of abuse at age five, which she then revealed for the first time to the general public. She had told her mother, and they had pressed charges, but a jury could not believe that the nice, kindly, strait-laced, old man could have done what he did.[3]

"More states must join those who obtain information on under-age-12 assaults, and the federal government simply must accept responsibility for gathering more data. An ugly and vicious wildfire rages in too many homes, and the "fire department" is not being notified.

"One measurement of the impact of incest came up in Washington. As many as 75% of female pornography performers are victims of incest or child sexual abuse, feminist writer Andrea Dworkin told the Attorney General's Commission on Pornography. Moreover, the profiteers of pornography in the U.S. alone make more money than the National Football League, Major League Baseball and National Basketball Association *combined*!

"The cycle of the abused becoming abusers is as high as 40%, and molested children experience higher levels of depression, drug and alcohol abuse, prescription drug dependency and emotional disturbances than occur in the population as a whole."[4]

In any case, this is no small matter. A top researcher, David Finkelhor, estimated more than 1,000,000 Americans walk around with the experience of *father-daughter incest alone*, and he estimated that new incidents occur at the rate of 16,000 per day! And that research was developed more than two decades ago. Incest is a fire out of control.[5]

"That does it!" I throw down the paper. I begin pacing the living room. "I am decided: I will no longer sit silent. So many voices say, 'Keep quiet. Keep the secret.' My Mother, my extended family, my lawyers

… If I tell the truth, someone might feel embarrassed … and sue!"

The societal pressure to keep incest swept under the rug makes me cringe and want to vomit. The silence provides sanctuary for the perpetrators of child sexual assault. No one, even millions who otherwise think of themselves as good people, wants the report … "Keep silent." Keeping silent is like having cancer and telling no one; yet speaking is like having AIDS and telling everyone.

"NO!" I shouted to the empty room. "I will not be silenced by shame any longer, no matter what they say, no matter what the outcome. As a child, I did not know how to speak up. But as an adult, I do, and I must."

When a subject is taboo for open and honest discussion without shame and disgrace, then the victims suffer alone in silence, and any sense of community remains ignorant and uncaring. I have learned how the silence eats away at lives and manifests itself in various addictions and self-destructive behavior – alcoholism, drug abuse, sexual abuse, gender confusion, generational abusive cycles, anxiety and depression, despair, and suicide.

Our society sometimes deals with the symptoms but rarely faces the root causes. We are told that, whether the violation took place once or repeatedly, its psychological damage is devastating.[11] The innocence is forever lost; you cannot be the person you were before the violation. For me, its full impact never goes away.

My passion is to expose the secrecy, to help set my fellow survivors free from the desperate silence, to invite God into the darkest places of our hearts and walk with us through healing and to neutralize the shadowy undertow that takes us down. I have learned that broken lives can be transformed by the power of a truly loving God. I have an urgency to help protect the next generation of potential victims, to help heal the hearts of the broken, and to be an audible voice for some important conversations each needs to have with themselves, with key persons in their families and with caring authorities in the medical and legal communities.

Any doubts I had about telling all were wiped away when I was called to jury duty on a rape case in metro Atlanta. Of the 36 prospective jurors, lawyers were hard-pressed to find 12 who had not been sexually molested as a child or who had known family or friends who experienced sexual assault as children. This gave me even more conviction to forge my way ahead. God seemed to be telling me in His own way that my voice needed to be heard, and I needed to become a voice for tens of thousands of victims. I want to teach victims to speak of their abuse and teach society how to receive the account.

Therefore, I am writing – fiercely and fast. This is more than a book to me. It is my Declaration of Freedom from bondage. It is my living proof that the past need not control me. It is my testimony of the faithfulness of God, no matter the awfulness of man. It is also my mission statement, for whatever else I may do in life, I want this message to go on helping others through their pain, their shame, their survival, and their victory. It has become my trumpet to sound a call to arms against both the evil of incest and the silence that gives it sanctuary.

For the flight through these pages, the reader will have to be ready for candor and raw honesty about a taboo topic. I am writing openly what many only dare to relive in private as they struggle through endless nights even to accept their own tragedy. My motives are not for shock and awe but to bring a difficult issue out of the dark shadows, to shed some light and understanding, to create compassion, to set aside the shame and disgrace for the survivors, and ultimately, to help in healing.

I want to urge the silent survivors whose wounds are deep as or deeper than mine to value themselves, to stand up, to speak up and, yes, to testify. Silence enables the injustice; silence is the enemy of healing; silence cooperates with evil and is the tool the enemy uses to keep so many in bondage; silence is not the answer.

At the risk of considerable and crushing embarrassment, I will try to be as candid as humanly possible. Of course, the names of persons, places, and settings have been changed to protect others. One word of caution: If you are a victim of incest, consult with a trustworthy and wise colleague as you begin reading. My story is my reality; it troubles me to fight through reliving the memories to be able to tell the story and recount the truth. This telling can be no less disquieting to other survivors of incest. While I urge them to tell their stories, they, of course, must do so at their own pace and in their own time as I have had to do. Without any reservation, I urge them to begin telling to a journal or diary, to a totally trustworthy adult or family member, to a national hotline (see directory in the Appendix) or to a trained counselor. Tell it! The telling is likely to be the pathway toward healing; it has been for me.

Personal experience helps define us. Therefore, we must fully embrace the need to talk about a difficult subject that paralyzes its victims. Generations of secrecy have destroyed lives, hopes, and dreams. The wounded among us now reach epidemic proportion, yet there are so few platforms for honesty and for healing.

As you join in this journey, join me also in vigilant prayer that these goals might come to pass in multiplied thousands of lives, all to the honor and praise of a gracious and loving Heavenly Father God who loves us exactly as we are and who has the power to move us into all He originally planned for us to be. That is my prayer; now this is my story. I confess I could not have re-lived and written it without my quiet time on the river.

CHAPTER 2

The Raging River

The car windows are rolled down and the cool morning wind blows my long black hair wildly. I've tried hard to pluck the grays as fast as they sprout, but in the rear-view mirror, I spot one standing straight up. I'm not ready for gray yet. My vanity emerges. The sun shines so brightly on the windshield, and I quiver inside with anticipation. I can't wait to get there. I haven't turned the stereo up so loud in years. I love this CD, "Touched by an Angel," and I've replayed "Testify to Love" six times since I left Birmingham. Its message clutches me:

All the colors of the rainbow.
All the voices of the wind.
Every dream that reaches out.
That reaches out to find where love begins.
Every word of every story.
Every star in every sky.
Every color of creation lives to testify.
For as long as I shall live I will testify to love.
I'll be the witness in the silences when words are not enough.
With every breath that I take I will give thanks to God above.
For as long as I shall live I will testify to love.[7]

I'm on an adventure to a place I've never been, literally and figuratively. My therapist has urged me for months to cut loose and go. She says I can't run from myself any longer. She says it's time to face my reflection in the mirror. In my early thirties, I began to unravel at the seams, emotionally and physically. The show could not go on. I began to systematically shut down. Intensive therapy seemed the only answer as I avoided commitment to a hospital. At that time, the phrase "mental hospital" seemed too scary. Now, after months of digging into my childhood, it is time for a sabbatical, a white-water rafting trip alone down the Chattooga River in an attempt to conquer my fears, to conquer my past, and to conquer myself.

I yearn for time alone, yet time alone frightens me. I yearn to find myself and to reconnect what I've spent years disconnecting. I am on an internal road trip. The thick trees are so green that they glow like velvet, and the clouds are white as cotton against the crisp blue sky. I play "picture the cloud," a game I loved as a child. I would lie flat in the backyard staring straight up to heaven determining what character was floating overhead. I found contentment in the simplest of pleasures. It was easy to spot Mickey Mouse, Winnie the Pooh, even a unicorn gracing my heavens.

The crisp June summer day is a gift, and I'm going to just think on all of its values all day. I've got to pay attention. I don't want to miss my exit. Anticipation is one of my most favorite emotions. Though I am very excited about the weekend ahead, I have tried so hard to suspend my expectations. I want to live in this moment.

The river is calling me, and I intend to drink in every ounce of serenity and revel in its rage. I will walk through the memories once and for all, and I will leave them on this river. The mountain will hold me up while the river cleanses me. I will fight the rapids for my life, I will fight the *memories for my life, and I will purge the rage within to break the undertow.*

The Taste of Fear

When I'm alone, when I drive through the pick-up window, when I'm waiting in line, when I soak in a hot tub, when I dream, memories come like a flood. I wish they would sprinkle my thoughts like morning dew on a fresh cut lawn. Instead, they stain my mind like grease and grime on white linen. I squeeze my eyes tight to forget, I squeeze my mind to extradite their horror, but the memories torment me, memories of when the fear invaded my life at the age of three.

"Mommy, it hurts."

"What hurts?"

"He hurts. He hurts me, Mommy."

"How does he hurt you?"

"He hurts me down there, Mommy."

"He does spank you pretty hard, but he just wants you to be a good girl. I've got to go to work. Mommy's got to make a living. Don't stick out your tongue, and just be a good girl today. Mommy loves you. Do the best you can, the best you can to behave. Bye."

"Mommy, please don't leave me here. Please Mommy, please Mommy, please don't go. No Mommy, no please ...."

The door slammed shut, and the secret was sealed. And with it, a weight, a weight at times too heavy for a three-year-old to bear, became an anchor on my spirit that became heavier with each passing year, causing me to sink deeper and deeper into the depths of despair. The secret swallowed my soul a million times over, a silent secret that altered my life forever.

My stepfather was 5-feet, 8-inches tall with a measly build and a receding hairline, short jet black hair that was always greased over to the right side, and a hallow face that showed no mercy. He wore false teeth and was rarely seen without them in his mouth. He would remove them when he slept, and the occasional glimpse made him look 90 years old. He was almost twenty years older than my Mother. His eyes were green and at times of rage, they would appear to sink into his head and turn tornado storm gray. His dark, leathery skin would turn from brown to red in zero to three seconds, and you would feel the presence of the devil. The lined crevices on his forehead and around his mouth would deepen when he turned inside out, and I could taste the fear in my mouth. An evil possessed him that drove his tongue to curse God with every breath. The other profanities, though harsh, never dominated his speech like "g-d." He hated people, he hated blacks, he hated relatives, except of course his own. He hated his job, he hated neighbors, and most of all, he hated me.

The oatmeal was before me and in a much larger bowl than a three-year-old could eat.

"I don't like oatmeal," I said. I shuddered at his immediate rage.

"Eat the g-d oatmeal now!" he bellowed. "When I walk back in this room it better be gone."

I began to shove the spoon in my mouth as fast as I could. Moments later, he returned, grabbed the spoon and fed me faster than I could swallow. I began to choke and vomit. I never vomited in his presence again; I learned quickly. I was so afraid, that I had to swallow. His perversion became my poison. I ingested an increasing dose of it daily. It not only poisoned my body, but also my mind and my soul.

I began to swallow pain like a pill. At the tender age of three, I knew I was swallowed by darkness and surrounded by evil. Being born in the '60s, at an idealistic time in our nation's history was unfortunate for me.

My real father met my Mother in college; he was her sweetheart from Day One. It was the first marriage for both of them. She saw in him all that she lacked in her own family rearing. From the outside looking in, they appeared well-to-do, a nice middle-class, red brick home in the center of a small town and hundreds of acres of farmland across the county line. His parents appeared to be happily married. They put on what many people did in the '60s: a front of perfection. Everyone wanted Camelot; few got it.

To this day, the sketchy details I really know about this man she married, this man who fathered me, is so dark and disappointing. He was appointed my father by God in heaven, but not once did he honor God or me, and not once did he do anything to deserve the title. His absence from my life and from my children's lives still baffles and troubles me.

When I was only days old, he walked away, washed his hands of me and never looked back. He, too, lives with his own giant, one that appears he has never been able to overcome. A short time after they were married, my Mother discovered that he had epilepsy. It controlled not only his ability to function, but also to hold down a job and be a stable provider and marriage partner. The disease apparently altered his personality and spun him into a tunnel of depression where he now resides. I keep waiting and hoping for a phone call, a card, or a visit, and it never comes. As an eternal optimist, I look for those acts, but the reasonable dream of a little girl for an engaged, loving Daddy remains unfulfilled.

They certainly looked happy in a picture I found as a child. That faded vintage photo became my treasure, and I kept it hidden in my dresser drawer. It was a 3"x5" black and white of my father carrying my Mother across the threshold after they were married. She wore her delicate white gloves and a perfect Jackie Onassis pill box hat with only a shadow of mesh covering her face. He was tall and solidly built - the body of a twenty-something-year-old. He had dark eyes and dark wavy hair with round cherry cheeks and a big smile that made him look approachable. I would study that picture for years to come, thousands of times, and ask myself what went wrong. Why did you leave us? Why did you turn your back on us? Where did you go? If you didn't love my Mother, why couldn't you love me? Why wouldn't you even try?

They married while both were still in college, and his parents helped them financially. They were both working on teaching degrees from a local university. The facts are fuzzy, but I know a teaching job for one or both took them to Florida where I was conceived. Their fragile union was not strong enough to withstand the challenges of life, and their love not mighty enough to face his epilepsy. He left, and shortly thereafter, she faced a tough reality: she was carrying his baby.

Apparently, wanting desperately to abandon all responsibility, he divorced her and divorced me at my birth. His entire family turned their backs on us, and I lived in hell only an hour away from them, never to lay eyes on my biological father or his family until 15 years later. Those would prove to be brutal years, facing one harrowing circumstance after another. His abandonment left a huge whole in my heart that I could only feel and never fill.

'I Do' ... He Did

After a brief meeting in a Laundromat and a two-week courtship, my Mother married a man I was immediately forced to call "Daddy" from the age of three. In hindsight, it seemed to me that my Mother was desperate for a mate and a father for me; she struggled with relationships. She tells me that memories of her childhood are blighted by events she can't remember, pain she dares not recall. She says she never felt wanted or loved and that somewhere in her childhood this limiting belief seems to have stolen her confidence.

Abuse comes in many disguises; abuse causes a pattern of feeling and of reacting. It drains your energy, shatters your joy. Abused persons don't stick up for themselves, much less anyone they love. I feel as though she was an easy target for our abuser. It seems he processed very quickly that he could control her (and subsequently control me) without much effort.

In the 1960s, society did not accept a single mother, especially a teacher who was an example for the next generation. She was a stunningly beautiful woman, with perfect features at 25, with short wavy blonde hair, big green eyes and exquisite facial features. She sported a perfect size 10 and had a sweet and innocent demeanor. I'm sure he quickly learned she was a decent woman who protected her virtue. I can almost see his devious mind clicking. He summed up all the pluses and set out to ruin our lives. I can only guess she was vulnerable, searching desperately for a husband and a father for me, so she quickly said, "I do."

And yet, part of my mind wonders: Did he see darkness in her that would feed the demons in him? Did he think that she would turn a blind eye? Who can fathom the psyche of a man who would-- who could-- physically, emotionally and sexually abuse a little girl or, worse yet, a mother who renders herself helpless in the situation? Was it nature or lack of nurture that turned a man into an animal? I wish I knew the darkness that loomed in his childhood, the secrets hidden in him to create such a sickness. I would bet my last dollar that he was abused somehow and in some way in his own rearing. He never spoke of his childhood, only that he was the baby of six children.

He was void of all decency but excellent at pretending we were a perfectly normal, middle-class family. They both worshiped material things, the very best money could buy. Name-brand junkies, you could call them. We were always surrounded with the most expensive and beautiful paintings, sofas, chairs, silk bedspreads, velvet pillows, and the finest clothes - only the best name brands would do. Yet, we were only a financially middle-class family struggling to make ends meet. They both had modest salaries; he was a blue-collar factory worker, and my Mother was a schoolteacher. They foolishly spent money and then sweated over the finances, because, of course, there was never enough money to pay bills. Had they lived within their means, we would have avoided the arguments over money and experienced some degree of peace.

On many days, he was my caregiver, while my Mother taught school. He ran a machine at a local factory and worked rotating shifts, either 3 p.m.-11p.m., 7 a.m.-3p.m. or 11 a.m.-7p.m. The exact times became my guide as to how I could peacefully live, and I would plan carefully so I could try to have truly free time to ride my bike or talk to a friend. He'd leave dressed in his stiff, blue, cotton uniform, and return with the sulfur smell of hell seeping through his pores. The plant discharged the sulfuric chemical fumes through their giant stacks, and this smell was poison to me. He hated his job and grumbled about everyone else's incompetence but his own. My Mother left me often with him, despite my pleas.

He played wicked mind games on me. He would manipulate situations when I was so young, I couldn't possibly understand what was going on. His goal was to prove I was a "bad little girl" and thus deserved the dish of humiliation he served me daily. On one occasion, I couldn't have been more than four; he left me in the car and dared me to get out, while he went shopping in Mobile. It was the heat of summer, and he knew I had to go potty. He left me in the back seat of the car for what seemed like hours and returned to find me drenched in sweat and gasping for air. He soon discovered a puddle of urine that I struggled to keep on the vinyl floor mat of his blue Challenger.

He pulled me out of the backseat by my hair, spanked me harshly and that evening reported to my Mother that the marks were on my legs were because I had been a bad girl and wet my pants. After holding it until I cried, I remember taking down my pink panties and trying so deliberately to wet only the vinyl mat. I was hot, scared and I had to go potty. Damned to punishment. He was evil incarnate. To me he was the devil.

He repeatedly put me in these damned-if-I-did and damned-if-I-didn't positions. He did this time and time again. He'd sit me down in front of the TV in a child's rocking chair and dared me to move until I desperately had to go. He'd force me to sit there for hours, struggling with the dilemma. Had to go; dared to move. It was more than a preschooler's mind could process. I was scared to get out of that chair: I was scared to sit and I was scared to wet my pants. I was a bad girl, damned either way, ultimately urinating from fear and exhaustion. His words were harsh. "You stupid little s--t." I trembled. He used this opportunity to touch me. His hands were wrong. His intentions were wrong.

Once I was cleaned up, and he was finished with me, I was taken to Joe's Hamburger Shack for a milkshake. Joe's was a hamburger joint that had drive-up window service in Gulf City, the next small town over toward Mobile. The milkshake tasted good, and I admired the waitresses who came out to the car with their frilled aprons and paper hats. That vanilla milkshake and the Joe's Hamburger Shack

26

entertainment made the secret taste better for a millisecond, yet the poison contaminated my soul.

He was calm afterward, and he would tell me he had to clean up my mess. He told me he wouldn't tell my Mommy I was bad and that I had wet my pants; he wouldn't tell her how he had to clean me up. He said if I told, she would spank me too, and I should never tell her. He asked me how much I liked milkshakes. I said it tasted good. Then we would roll through the drive-through at the bank while he made his weekly paycheck deposit, and he would get me a red sucker because, he said, "I was such a good girl". The sweet taste of the sucker eased the confusion of hours past; the words "good girl" replaced the words "bad girl." Sweets became my pacifier, confusion my compromise.

CHAPTER 3

The Ring

I turned into the drive of the only restaurant I had passed for miles. I was famished. It was an old, tin-roof house where each room was crowded with red checked cloth tables and green vinyl leather and chrome chairs. Above my table hung several weathered old black and white pictures in oval dark wood antique frames from generations past, generations that looked like they had nothing to smile about judging by their stoic grimaces. I gazed into their hollow eyes to see myself staring back in the reflection of the glass. I wonder what secrets lay hidden behind those eyes, what pain they endured. Not one corner of their mouths were turned up, not one eye lifted in joy. The eyes are the windows to our soul.

I sat in the corner and was so excited to spot pork barbeque on the menu, my favorite. I was soon gobbling down a huge barbeque sandwich with Brunswick stew, fries and a quart jar full of syrup sweet ice tea. It was a local hangout and probably one of only a couple in this small town of Long Creek. I looked up with a smile at the locals as they walked by. Each one would stare, trying to read my story written on my face, perhaps curious as to why I was here alone. My forehead probably read "Desperate for Deliverance."

That was the purpose of my voyage. I enjoyed every bite of lunch and once again reveled in that soothing, satisfying feeling of having my stomach full. I've battled my weight for years, never seeming to shed the insulation that protects me. I know it's because I find so much comfort in food.

I reach in my pocket for some cash to pay, and I feel the ring. I pull it out and stare at the sapphires, pressing my fingers over the sharp prongs until it hurts. Suddenly, the memories flood my mind, memories of a Christmas long ago. It was usually a happy time as we cooked large meals, visited our relatives in the country, received an adequate stash from Santa under the tree, and he was decent for that day. It was a day of reprieve, for he never touched me on Christmas, my real Christmas present.

Ironic 'Gift'

For this my 15th Christmas, I hadn't really asked for anything but clothes, and lacked any excitement about the season, as the thrill of Santa had long passed. At that stage in my difficult teenage years, joy had eluded me. That morning, I remember looking under my side of the Christmas tree to a very slim offering. I stuck my lips out and scooped up my few items while my sisters could barely comb through their piles. We always got tangerines and candy canes in our stocking, and I was not eager to empty it. After all the commotion had ended, my stepfather, Carl, asked me why I hadn't emptied my stocking. I told him I had felt the tangerines and candy canes. He insisted I dump it on the floor. There lay a little, gray, velvet box from Service Merchandise, and in it sparkled a diamond and sapphire ring. I didn't want to put it on.

Ironically, the prongs snagged every piece of clothing I wore, and that had been my cover story for not wearing it at the time, or so I told myself. It was beautiful and I hated it. The ring was a symbol of silence.

The ring is still not on my finger, but why am I carrying it? I squeeze the ring tightly, slip it back into my jeans, and turn my focus to the river again.

Life as the Bad Girl

I would hold my breath until his next moment of opportunity. He would snatch the leather belt from his loops and sling it off uncontrollably. Sometimes, it would hit my head, then my stomach, then my legs. If I didn't cry hard enough, he would turn the belt around and fling the buckle at me until I was curled up in a ball.

I dared not run. When I ran, the beatings lasted much longer. Running was just one more reason to beat me. I ran out of a natural instinct to flee his tirades and the beatings. He considered my flight dishonoring; he considered me shielding my legs with my hands disrespectful, so he would hold my hands while he whipped me. To him, it was his right to beat me; to him, it was his right to do whatever he wanted; to him, it was his right to treat me like an animal. I belonged to him for whatever he pleased. "Please Daddy, please, please stop," I begged. He would touch me after the violent outrages, sickly consoling me. "If you're a good girl I won't have to whip you, so now you have to be a good girl. Just sit still, and let me touch you; I'll show you how to be a good girl," he would then purr.

After he finished using me, he would brush my long black hair and tell me over and over that this was our secret, and if I dared to tell anyone, ever, I would be taken away, and no one would ever find me. How could I know I was trapped in a sick world of suffocating silence? I was caught in a downward spiral, robbed of my innocence before I knew what was happening. I was robbed of my childhood's joy because the secret never left me. The mind control was so gradual I didn't even know when it started, how to stop it, or how to say "no." The secret, now firmly planted, only grew in my mind, creating walls like a maze, a wicked web I could never escape. The secret changed me. It turned me into a survivor; it tormented me. I felt perverted. It changed how I perceived myself and the forces around me. Every hour of every day was spent swallowing the secret. She, the little girl inside me, tried so desperately to process the hurt. He hurt me. He turned me inside out. He hurt my mind and my heart. He damaged my normal development all for his sick pleasure. His perversion became the poison I would have to swallow almost every day.

I was sacrificed. And my Mother looked the other way, never wanting to look at me, never wanting to see. If she ever looked into my eyes, she would have seen the agony and pain. But she seemed so self-absorbed in her own turmoil that I was never her priority. Did she count her financial security more important than my safety? She must have convinced herself it really wasn't that bad. His rampages were often followed by sweet talk and more branded purchases to console my Mother, followed by more abuse, until it became a vicious cycle. She tried to convince me it really wasn't that bad, because it wasn't seven days a week, twenty-four hours a day, but fifty to seventy-five per cent of the time. The lesson was that we could tolerate this amount of torment in our lives in exchange for all that he provided, because after all, he was a "good provider."

It seemed everyone thought I was a cute princess with a perfect life. On the outside, they saw a pretty, little girl with big dark eyes, soft porcelain white skin, lightly freckled round nose, and long black hair that hit my waist, with cropped bangs slightly above my brow. Most of the time, my Mother dressed me up like a little doll. Everywhere we went, people commented that I was an adorable child. A "china doll," they would say. Back then, it was a weekly ritual to truck to the beauty parlor on Thursday afternoons. I would beg and plead to go. My Mother would get her weekly beehive hair-do. Fanatic about keeping it in place, she wouldn't wash it, and she would sleep stiff-necked rather than lay her head on the pillow at night – until the following week! I remember one afternoon, when I was about five years old, she dressed me in my Health-Tex matching short set, and the other ladies in the beauty parlor made a fuss over me. One of the other customers, Miss Sally, perched under the dryer, put her hand over her mouth in horror, and politely asked, "What in this world are those stripes doing on the back of that precious little one's legs?"

My Mother faced the mirror while her hair was teased into the beehive and politely replied, "If she acted as pretty as she looked, we wouldn't have a problem. Her Daddy is strict and punishes her harshly."

That would be the phrase she used for years to come; it became her mantra. "Her Daddy is just strict with her." But he was not strict; he was brutally mean.

She consoled herself that the physical abuse she allowed me to endure was okay. She herself didn't feel the burn. She didn't feel the embarrassment of people looking at her legs. She had to console herself that it was for my own good. She feared him. At that time, what was done behind closed doors was nobody's business but your own. No Department of Family and Children's Services to call, no teacher interference, no neighbor concern, only a complacency to accept what was. Especially in a small town, people were expected to mind their own business if they didn't want trouble.

In Port Logan, a bedroom suburb of Mobile, everyone minded his own business. No one wanted trouble, especially not with Carl Rivers. The kids would egg our house, and he would wait on the roof with the shotgun cocked for their next attack. They loved to taunt him, at least monthly, and he toted his gun up to watch for them. He would shout strings of profanity at them. At least once, I remember him firing over their heads. His reputation preceded him, and everyone knew he was mean as a snake. They could hear the profanity echo through our open windows. They could see the veil of darkness that surrounded our house. If they kicked or tossed a ball into our yard, they were too afraid of Carl to retrieve it.

So Many Secrets

The first day of kindergarten was hard, but the second day was harder. I knew I was different from all the other five-year-old girls. I believe this was a time when I began to abandon my own self in search of who I wanted to be - a normal little girl without a millstone tied around her neck. I did whatever I had to do to be accepted at home, by my classmates and by my teachers. I loved school. I remember that sick feeling when it was time to line up to go home. Since my Mother taught school, and in those days kindergarten was only half day, I had to spend the afternoon with "Daddy."

Some afternoons, after kindergarten let out, we would go on long rides, thirty minutes or so, on the outskirts of town, where he would visit his mistress. They would sit me down in front of the TV while they retreated to the bedroom. I would see her out of the corner of my eye, half-dressed down to her girdle, going to the kitchen to get something out of the cabinet. If she ever caught me peeking at her, she would snap, "Turn your head and watch TV."

In a while, he would return, load me in the car, and all the way home he would repeat, "This visit is our secret. You know what I'll do to you if you say a word. Not a word, do you understand me. If your Mother asks, we were shopping."

We stopped at the 7-11, and he bought me a bag of M&M's. No wonder I developed an art for lying. I was taught at such a young age, and then severely punished for lying when it didn't cover his evils.

School was a place where I could escape the pain, a place where I felt nurtured. The time away from the madness was my salvation. I was a bright child who could quickly win my teacher's heart, and I soon figured out how to become the teacher's pet. In kindergarten, I was voted Valentine Queen by my peers. I felt very special that day. I liked that feeling: the popularity, the attention, the competition. This may have been the birth of my drive, my determination. I developed an innocent crush on a boy in kindergarten class. Of course, Carl couldn't see the innocence of it all and began to call me a "little slut," at the age of five.

When we look in the rear-view mirror of life, so often the bad overshadows the good, and the sad overshadows the joy. Maybe it's because the pain we experience as children is seared on our hearts forever. Maybe the intense emotions scar us and change us in ways we can't explain and in ways we can't reverse. There were days of joy in my youth and a very few days I never wanted to end. I had an enormous imagination and, like most kids, loved to watch TV. I would pretend I was the star. "I Love Lucy" was my all-time favorite show. It taught me how to laugh out loud, how to be silly and how to manage in a world out of my control. Lucy always managed in a world out of her control. Every predicament she faced with tears, then with laughter, then tears. I tried hard to laugh. I would immerse myself in TV shows, such as "Gilligan's Island," "The Carol Burnett Show," "The Brady Bunch." These were my favorites because they would make me laugh and provide a moment of escape.

Carl soon learned how much I loved TV, and he would ban me from watching when I was 'bad.' He would send me to my child's table in the kitchen behind the refrigerator to sit like a robot and play with my doll that I hated and my tea sets. I would shove spoonfuls of pretend-food into my doll's mouth. I was forced to "play" this "game" which I detested. It was not what a child would consider "play" at all. I would peer around the refrigerator to watch what was on TV, and he would hear me laugh and rush to give me a smack across the face. "Don't hit her in the face," Mother would scream, and then he would turn on her and give her a nice shove. But I continued to laugh, even if on the inside. Laughter was the only medicine for my wounds. That was a lesson I learned early: laugh long and hard every chance you get because you don't know when the opportunity will come again. Carl could be coming ...

I loved those long summer days when Carl was away at work, and I could play all day in old clothes. My very best friend, Cindy, lived nearby down a dead-end street. But I was never allowed to step foot outside of my yard. It was a real treat when Cindy would come over to play. My Mother would give us a huge bag of clothes, and we would build castles out of sheets, dress up, and go to far-away places while lost in make-believe. We would play house and create a place where all was happy and peaceful. My make-believe world was a wonderful one that I could create and control. It was so unlike my real world.

We lived in a small, white-brick house with black shutters. It was a modest ranch home with three small bedrooms and two small baths perched on a huge corner lot on a dead-end street. I know it was economical to live in Port Logan, because the morning trains' whistles would blast right behind our house, and it was in the path of the airport, which brought rumbling jets overhead. What irony that the noise outside couldn't compete with the turmoil inside. Mother slaved to keep the house spotlessly clean. No one was ever allowed inside, not playmates, not friends, and rarely family. Shoes were to be removed, and you didn't sit on the couch, chairs, or the bedspreads. Your hands and feet were never clean enough to be placed anywhere. Our home was kept meticulous but only for looks, not for living. You weren't allowed to mess it up, because "he worked hard" for all these beautiful things. The beautiful things were a symbol of his success. We were a symbol of his accomplishment.

Carl loved to landscape and work in the yard, so we had the prettiest yard around. From a very young age, I remember spending hours visiting nurseries, picking out only the perfect plants and working hand in hand with him to place them accurately in his masterpiece. There were pink azaleas that surrounded the acre-yard like a moat, green shaved boxwoods under all the windows, and palm trees symmetrically planted in the front corners surrounded by junipers.

There was a rose garden precisely shaped in a triangle in the back corner with blooms of every color. We labored for weeks building a frame for a huge grape vine in the back left corner of the yard where a plum tree was planted next to it beside a large stump. There were pear trees and pecan trees scattered throughout the back yard along with two huge pines in the front. I spent many hot days keeping the yard weed-free and manicured. He was neurotic about everything. Order was his stronghold, perfection his idol.

Once, my cousin Greg spent the weekend. Greg and I were very close. He had fireball-red hair and a specked, freckled nose. We shared so much in common. We loved to play games, we loved to read, and we loved art; but more importantly, we were both suffering from abuse and bonded in our pain. Carl was always so nasty to Greg when no one was around. He would accuse us children of vulgar play.

I believe Carl was jealous because we shared an innocent cousin kinship. On one particular day, Greg was at our house for a rare visit. We were having a ball playing outside, and our entrepreneurial spirit led us to open a general store. We needed "play" money, so we got the prize idea to strip the leaves off the trees and use the bright green leaves as our money for our store. Our store was doing well, so we needed hundreds of leaves. When Carl discovered the leaves gone and the naked limbs on his precious pear trees, he stripped the limbs and switched both our legs, yelling profanity to the top of his lungs. Greg never wanted to come back to our house and play after that. Greg never wanted to be around Carl again. He trembled at the thought of Carl.

When I dissect myself, I see so clearly how the torture and abuse mauled and molded me. From the fragile age of four, I was put outside with a bucket to weed the flowerbeds. The time I spent laboring with those weeds gave me time to dream, time to sing, time to feed my soul with the freshness of the soil. I started at one corner of the house in the early morning with orders to continue around the whole house until I got back to the same spot. It was like asking me to cross the Mojave Desert, but I worked diligently without complaint.

Complaining was not tolerated; complaining only brought a hoe-handle lash across my back. As the sun floated higher in the sky, sweat began to pour. I would stop to ask for some water, and my Mother would direct me to the outside water spigot at the back door. I can still taste the hot water that first sprang forth until the lukewarm water flowed. The heat outside was intense, and I soon learned to spray my face with the water hose. But for lunch, she would make me a fried bologna sandwich on white bread with extra mayo, my favorite. I couldn't come inside to eat because I was too dirty. I would find a shady spot under the pine tree and eat my sandwich alone quietly whispering my fears to Ms. Beasley, my favorite doll, because she listened intently.

There was a metal blue and white-striped swing set that I could play on when I finished. I would work tenaciously, knowing my reward was waiting. Finally, as the crickets would sound, I'd be finished. When I pulled the last weed, I would run like the wind to my swing and swing until the sun went down. I can still hear the crickets chirping and see the lightning bugs appear as I'd race to catch them. I can feel the smile on my face. I had been a good girl that day. I had done all that I was told, and I got to swing. It was a great day; he left me alone that day. "Angela, it's time to come inside." I'd get a warm bath, eat supper, maybe even watch an Elvis movie, and then snuggle in bed with a kiss from my Mom.

CHAPTER 4

The Reign of Evil

Power: physical and verbal power were the reins he used for control; it was a power by fear, a trembling fear that made sweat bead and seep through my pores like blinding raindrops. He took power over me by eliminating things I loved and forcing me to do things I detested. He seized power over simple things, like my crayons, which I treasured. I loved to color, and a new clean coloring book filled me with exhilaration. Mommy would color with me, and I loved to share that time together coloring. I would only have to turn over a slightly less than perfect paper from school, perhaps a B+, and he would take great joy breaking my crayons. Then he would take my coloring books away as punishment. It was an easier punishment than when he beat me, but it was painful nonetheless, and my tears would well up.

I loved my crayons, especially new ones, and he attempted to break my spirit with those crayons. He came close many times, but he never succeeded. He scared me to the bone with pain that sometimes was too hard to bear. I learned to hide my coloring books, and I learned to lie about my less- than-perfect grades. In second grade, I was a master at turning a C into an A or B, a master at his signature and a master at manipulation. I maneuvered my world to maintain my sanity, to preserve my soul, and to survive. I was such a little girl with such a big burden.

If you know this fear, if you identify with surviving, if you too developed a dark side to manipulate your madness, please know it is because you did not have power. Neither you nor I had any control over our circumstances. I was a little girl gripping the defense mechanisms and survival modes needed to make it through the day. I was taught to lie so well that I lost the truth. I lost the truth within myself, and lost a consciousness to know better. The trauma initiates a chaos inside you and inside your world, a tumult that you can't live with and you can't live without. The chaos inside my mind grew and grew to an astronomical proportion.

There were few places where I felt safe, where I felt a diminished probability that he would break into a tirade, where I felt a reprieve from the cursing, the yelling, and the violence. Our house, though very small and very middle class, was decorated to a T. We had only the best-name furniture, only the fanciest of couches and chairs, and only original signed oils adorned the walls. Granted, we could never sit on our couches, wear our shoes inside, or eat anywhere but at the table. When they weren't looking, I would jump on the bedspreads and throw the silk pillows into the air. It was my brief moment of rebellion.

The process of decorating the tiny palace was like a savior to me, the process of going from Haverty's to Ethan Allen to Furniture Outlets in cities and nearby small towns. I would love our Saturday shopping sprees. Every furniture store clerk reassured me I was as pretty as a china doll. I had so much fun climbing on one velvet couch after another, moving from showroom to showroom looking at all the beautiful bedroom suits, paintings, artificial flower arrangements, and statues. I remember statues were the entire craze at that time, and we owned several. The bust of Jacob and the watering girl stone statues guarded the formal living room. I pretended I was in Greece or Italy or Spain, as I admired the artwork, soaking in the colors and the beautiful sculptures, playing a grown-up traveling the world. What irony. We would bring all the perfect furnishings into what the world saw as a perfect show of a home, when in actuality it was a shell of torture. The magnitude of it all seemed unbearable.

By the time I was six, he made me believe that all fathers made their little girls feel good by touching them. In a sick way, I enjoyed it when he didn't hurt me. He could be tender in his assaults. He would kiss me and hold me. That was so much better than hitting me with the belt or the shovel or whatever weapon he could grab. It was so much better than the days he made me march to the bathroom and pull down my panties, as I quivered. He would raise his arms above his head and lash the belt on my bottom, on my legs, his face blood red with rage, as he bawled how much he hated me.

When his arm tired, he would grab me by the back of the neck and hold my head in the toilet and flush. I would gasp for air. I can still smell the chlorine water in the toilet bowl. I can still feel the burn on my legs, I can still taste the salty tears in my mouth, and I can still hear my Mother screech, "Stop it, Carl, you're going to kill her! She hasn't done anything wrong. Please stop! God, please stop, she's just a little girl, and she can't take much more. You're going to kill her! I hate you, I hate you, Carl!" And then he would turn on her. He had all the power; he had total control. I dreaded my fatal marches to the bathroom.

Struggling in the Sewer

My deception skills soon sprouted like a sunflower seed and grew tall and strong. Wanting to stay out of trouble, but wanting more to keep out of his grip and away from the perversion, I kept finding myself in constant trouble. Yet, I continued to reach for the sky, exactly like the sunflower.

One cool, rainy morning, as a drizzle fell outside, I was a sleepy seven-year-old. He had worked the night shift and was coming in the door as my Mother was leaving for her teaching job. As usual, it was his job to get me breakfast and onto the bus before he went to sleep for the day. My Mother owned a lazy streak a mile long and a mile wide. She preferred giving me a candy bar and a kiss goodbye for breakfast. Laziness was a crime to Carl for which there was no pardon. He fixed my bowl of oatmeal, and I ate quickly. He was grumpy from his night's work and was yelling at me that I better not miss the bus. I was in second grade, and I already knew the routine if I missed the bus, so I tried to rush. I grabbed my book bag and ran as fast as I could to the bus stop just in time to see the blinking red lights and yellow flash disappear around Fontaine Drive.

I looked at the endless road ahead. I couldn't walk to school. I looked back at 465 Briar Patch Place at the corner lot where we lived knowing I couldn't walk home. I looked down into the dampness and saw a huge, round concrete sewer pipe. I crawled inside

45

that sewer pipe, and the tears poured down my face. I wiped my eyes with my long black hair. I was so scared. I finally stopped the faucet of tears and decided I would stay very still inside that pipe until the bus came home, and then I would walk home, arriving on schedule.

I knew what I'd have to face anyway that day, and I could not face it right then. Besides, I felt safe inside the concrete sewer pipe. I was cold; I was wet; I was scared, but it was the best alternative a seven- year-old could plan, one of the endless number of no-win predicaments my mind had to face. After what seemed like hours, when I couldn't stay curled up inside anymore, I squirmed out of the tight quarters. I had no idea how long I'd been in there. I reached for the sky to stretch for only a second; and my intent was to get right back inside the sewer pipe, when a car turned down the street and spotted me. I was busted.

It was Carl, and trouble again surrounded me like a mountain. I couldn't climb up it, over it, or around it. He insisted I intentionally missed the bus to skip school. If I ever did tell the truth, no one heard me. I was always a liar, a scammer, a manipulator. I didn't have a voice, even though the very existence of words tried to redeem me. I began a dialogue inside my head. I spoke words to myself no one ever heard. I only screamed inside my mind, so I was the only one to hear. I lost the power of screaming audibly. Besides the mental torment, Carl made sure my physical punishments were severe.

Twice Abandoned

Though pain weakens many, I found power in my pain. It was a power that penetrated past the tears to

46

a place of consolation, a place where my dreams kept me alive, kept me forging forward. It was an enormous power that I couldn't even really identify at the time. Now I know that source was God. If I could bottle and sell it, I'd be a millionaire. Yet God offers it as a gift, ready for the taking.

The harder I was beaten down, the higher I was determined to rise inside. I knew that somehow, some way, someday, my circumstances would change. I began a ritual of wishing on every birthday candle for a happy family. Like most families I knew, it was a tradition in our home to celebrate birthdays with a pretty, white-icing cake, candy roses and candles. As the candles were lit and the tune of "Happy Birthday" sung, I would begin to pray, to repeat a thousand times, "Please God, I wish, I wish, I wish for a happy family. Please hear my wish, I wish for a happy family. Please help me find my real father. Please give me a happy family that would share peace and joy. Oh please, oh please, oh please." The song would be well over and the screams of "just blow out the candles" would wake me from my daze. This was my only chance once a year to make a wish, so I had to make it count. Many years the candles would have almost burned out by the time I blew.

I thought that one day my real father would return and take us away. I cherished the image of him and my Mother in that little, wrinkled black and white photo that I carried with me, along with the sketchy details my Mother provided. That image was a vague shadow in my mind, a fantasy of a father I yearned for, a father who would love me innocently and wholesomely, a father who would treat me like a princess, a father I could take joy in calling "Daddy."

Birthdays came too slowly, so I decided to celebrate with every day's first evening star. I would gaze up into the heavens, fix my eyes on that twinkling diamond and recite, "Star light, star bright, I wish I may, I wish I might, have this wish I wish tonight. I wish for a happy family." I spoke the words fast before any other stars peeked through the dusk of evening. Somehow, that ritual comforted me. I believed in wishes, I believed in dreams, and I believed in prayer. That belief was all I had to cling to, and so I held it tightly.

One day my Mother was brushing out the knots in my long, thick black hair that hung barely above my waist, and I asked her why my name was different. It was seldom we had these moments of peace and quiet. "Why is your last name different than mine?" my curiosity bubbled. "All my friends have the same last names as their mommies and daddies." She began to tell the story of how she was married to my real father for a brief time, and when I came along, he didn't want us anymore. He didn't want the responsibility of a family. I knew then that the small black and white photo was of my real father. She confirmed my suspicion. I always suspected that Carl wasn't my *real* father, and the confirmation was a relief. His blood didn't run through my veins, and though it was not much consolation to cling to, it was something.

I asked the normal questions about my real father, "Is he the man in that picture in the top drawer of the armoire in my bedroom? What's his name? What does he look like? Where does he live? Will I ever see him? Why did he leave us?" My Mother told me how my grandmother, my biological father's mother, picked him up in north Florida and drove him back to his Alabama hometown leaving my Mother alone during her pregnancy. She said she only saw him one more time after that. When I was born, she dolled me up in a frilly red velvet dress and took me to see him in hopes he would reconsider his responsibility. He held me for under a minute and returned me, saying he didn't want to have anything to do with us. I would later learn that he made several futile attempts in my early years to connect with me.

It wasn't until I became an adult that I learned from a relative that his family had been riddled with alcoholism and abuse. He suffered in the crossfire of his own father's drunken outrages, and maybe that led to his decision to walk away. Maybe it was his physical health, the epilepsy, which made him feel unable to be a nurturing father. At times, I have felt it was all my fault. There was something in me he rejected. I have to believe for my own sanity that it wasn't me at all and that he had only selfish reasons for abandoning his own daughter. I have to believe it was more of his iniquity than it was mine.

My Mother said he left because he didn't want children, and I believed her and converted those words into torturous blame that played over and over in my head like a broken record. To me, it was my fault. What child at the age of seven doesn't believe her Mother? Whom else does a little girl have to trust? Who else is there to brush her hair and zip up her dress? Who else is there to kiss her goodnight and give her a hug? I had no one else to believe, and I couldn't hurt her with the secret. I was determined to seal it, knowing the silence would protect her, and her marriage, which to me seemed a bitter and disgusting dependency. I didn't know how to formulate the words. I didn't even know how to put into words what he did to me. I even blamed myself for Carl's cruel hand upon me. To this day, the little girl who still cries inside me knew that his actions were a terrible, horrific secret that would destroy her. I never conceived that a Mother could know and still coldly look the other way. I, like many sexually abused children, laid all the blame squarely on my own shoulders. Somehow, I thought, this had to be *all* my fault.

Abandoned. Now that was a big word for a seven-year-old to swallow. I felt abandoned by two people: my real father and my Mother. I don't believe my Mother really comprehended the irreparable damage she caused, and I don't think she comprehended the pain I felt and carry with me to this day. Even though she told me she loved me and wanted me from the moment she discovered she was pregnant, somehow those words bounced off me like rubber. She stood by and watched the daggers thrown at me and showed no strength in protecting me. My Mother told me she loved me many times, but she never made him stop. She never protected me from his hand; she never proved her love with her actions. She often left me alone with him despite my pleas. Deep down, I questioned her love for me. She said "love" with her words but never with her actions.

If I had only known what my innocent question would cause, I would have remained quiet. The whispering started immediately, as well as the long discussions behind closed doors. I only heard bits and pieces, and to small ears, words like "adoption," "attorney," "judge," and "court" caused great confusion. I didn't dare ask questions for fear I would say the wrong word in the presence of Carl and be punished. It was a constant struggle to get through dinnertime without angering him. I can remember him lunging at me across the table. His favorite lash was to stick me with his fork. If my elbows ever touched the table, he would pierce my arms with his fork and follow it up with, "I said get your *g-d* elbows off the table." I would smile inside and repeat to myself, "You're not my real Daddy." I always ate quickly and tried to disappear into the paneling.

They didn't explain very much, other than "he would be going to the courthouse tomorrow for you to be adopted, and then we'll take you on to school." We woke up early, I don't remember the month, but the morning was crisp, and I was dolled up in my prettiest dress. I tried to ask questions, but they had no interest in answering. Only the brief explanation, "Your Daddy is going to adopt you and give you his name."

Did anyone ever care that I'd rather have jumped on a spear face first than have his name? My questions pounded in my head, one after another, "How would my Daddy, my real Daddy ever find me if I didn't have his name? Could a piece of paper make Carl Rivers my real Daddy?" I could always rationalize in my young mind that he wasn't really my father, and that was the reason he was so mean to me. It felt good to know we weren't genetically connected.

I remember a huge, quiet, cold room, and lots of whispers. They kept me in the judge's chambers while they completed the paperwork. Afterward, I walked out as Angela Rivers with the last name Wells deleted from my life. Days later, I would learn that I was kept in that room because *he* was there. He, my real father, was there to sign the adoption papers. He was there; he was so close to me, and yet, he didn't even want to see me, to hug me, to touch me, to acknowledge me. He coldly signed me away to the devil.

More confusion set in as the next day I had to write my name differently at school. Though it may sound silly now, there was an intense grieving in my heart, a feeling that I wasn't the same person, a need still to write "Wells" in secret. I was only seven and barely learning to write in cursive. Some papers would come in the mail months later with "Wells." I'd simply forget, but he soon erased "Wells" from my mind with the consequences. Wells became a dirty word never to be spoken again. It changed me. I can remember the day I decided to change my name from Angela to Angie, as Carl always called me Angela. I answered to both names up until my teen years, when I totally abandoned Angela. Even though Angela was my God-given name, I didn't think it fit me anymore. It was too akin to Angel, which made me think of how unholy and dirty I felt.

Days of Humiliation

My new baby sister was brought home from the hospital, and she was more than a welcome distraction from the days of hostility. At least, until the night I messed up. When Carl arrived home at 11 p.m., I would still be up, because I seldom had a bedtime. One night he went straight to the new baby, picked her up and her loosely pinned diaper fell off. Mother laughed and proceeded to tell him I had changed her while she was in the bath. All hell broke loose, and he started swearing and beating me. He ranted and raved about how I could have stuck her with the pins and injured her. He was more irate at my Mother who, by now, was used to his tirades. I went to bed knowing that he had more punishment for me the next day. He assured me I would NEVER forget this lesson, and I assure you, I can barely write down what he did to me.

He woke me up very early. As I was wiping the sleep from my eyes, he stripped off all my clothes, pinned a diaper on me and pulled me out to the front yard where my bicycle sat. He forced me to ride my small bicycle on the grass in the front yard all day. I could barely pedal through the thick Bermuda grass, and I was naked and cold, except for the cloth diaper that covered my private parts. The kids in the neighborhood would walk by slowly, point, and laugh at me. People would slow as they drove past and stared hard. The humiliation was nauseating. Any dignity I had was gone. I was so ashamed, and riding that bicycle was so hard that I had to stand up from the seat to make each turn of the pedal. My Mother kept screaming, "That's enough, Carl!" But it was never enough until he said it was enough, for he held all power and all control. Her pleas were always ignored.

From that day on, I was scared to touch the baby. I didn't even want to look at her. My Mother wouldn't stop him, couldn't stop him. He enjoyed being cruel to me. He was insane, and I was his hobby.

CHAPTER 5

The Scream

En route to the river, and usually wherever I go, I discover the best food in the dumpiest places. This was no four-star venue, but lunch was delicious. Barbeque is one of my favorite foods and I have stuffed myself. I climb in my Ford Explorer feeling full, content and free as a bird, a bird newly released from its cage. I want to soar, but my wings are weighted with years of abuse. So I'm off to find the bed and breakfast where I'll be spending the weekend.

I continue on my internal road trip, slowing the car down so I can admire a creaky, old, rusty, red-iron bridge. Perched on the other side of the river sits a quaint, smallish, white house with black shutters, lace curtains peeking from the windows, and a big front porch, where I will spend the next two nights. I smirk at the coincidence of it being a little white house with black shutters – the very image of the house I want to leave behind. As I make my way across the bridge, I smile and wonder how many people have crossed over to the other side. Then I wonder if I'll ever be able to traverse the rusty bridge in my soul.

The innkeeper welcomes me into her cozy world with a big smile. She's a jolly, short, round, gray-haired woman with an apron tied around her waist. You can tell she is living her dream.

Her smile is infectious, and she is deliberate about showing me every room in the house, proudly explaining the heritage of each cherished antique. The house warms my spirit with its character and charm and eclectic décor. We quickly bond, and she dares ask the question.

56

"Do you have family or friends joining you?"

I reply, "No Ma'am, just me."

"All alone?" she asks.

"Yes Ma'am, I'm all alone."

Her curiosity gets the best of her and she probes on. "Are you going down the Chattooga by yourself tomorrow?"

"Yes, I'm on a sabbatical," I go on to explain, barely knowing the true meaning of the word sabbatical. "I have some baggage to deal with that I want to throw in the river, and life is too busy at home to get rid of it there. I figure if I go to the edge I can throw it over and be rid of it forever."

She smiles as if she knows exactly what I mean, but tells me, "Sometimes, the river throws it back."

The river sings in the background and begins to whisper my name. I shiver with excitement when I think of the adventure I've signed up for tomorrow. I'm shown to my tiny room with daybed, both clean and cute. Some other guests arrive. A mom and three teenage daughters check-in, and we politely greet each other. I settle in my small, humble accommodations, and the afternoon is mine. Wow, an afternoon with no kids, no husband, no agenda, no fear-- just freedom. I'm free to dance.

The river whispers a soothing tune, and the day calls me. The innkeeper points me in the direction of nearby Chaw Chaw Park. This park, she has informed me, is a great place for hiking and to enjoy several waterfalls. That sounds perfect. I find the park and wander around for hours. I chase butterflies, admire the wildflowers, and close my eyes, focusing on the sound of the river. All my senses are alert. I focus intently on the white caps in the flow of the river. I spot fish searching for a morsel of food. I take *my shoes off and wade in the painfully freezing water. I see fool's gold in abundance glittering under my feet. I sit on a giant bolder and watch the waterfall spray over the rocks to a whirlpool below. I remember a verse from my quiet time that week, "The water I give you will become in you a spring of water welling up to eternal life." John 4:13.*

There is so much welling up inside of me. I've swallowed hard and deep for so many years. I've swallowed the pain that my old friend, fear, has fed me. I've swallowed the vomit when there was room for no more pain. Now I'm choking.

I wander down trails, hiking up one hill and back down over rocks, always keeping the river in sight. I have seen plenty of western movies where no one ever got lost when they followed the river. The sound of the raging Chattooga River is a constant, like the rage I feel in my soul, buried in my very being. Suddenly, it hurls up from my gut, and I cannot contain it any longer. I start to scream at the top of my lungs. The screams echo off the hills. I run and I scream. I cry harder than I have ever cried. I sob until I lose my breath. I heave away the pain shoved down my throat for so many years.

My Papa

Growing up, I would have to say my Granny and Papa were my favorite people. They lived in the country on lots of land in a small red brick home inherited from my Granny's family. Her family was a bit disappointed with her choice in a husband. She was from money, and, according to her, she was destined to marry money. The family's dreams were destroyed when she married my Papa. But Granny, being the rebel that she was, married for love, not money, and she never regretted her decision. She was a grounding force in my life. I remember her gathering all the grandchildren on her feather bed and telling us stories of a headless ghost that drove the wagon through the fields. My cousins and I would tremble with fear as she painted the scene of her first encounter with the enigma, carefully describing what she was wearing, how she felt, and how the fear gripped her. We all sank into the center of the bed as she told the story that scared us to the bone. Somehow she managed to wrap her arms around all of us and, even with the scary story, we felt strangely safe.

Granny loved us dearly and sought to keep us entertained. She was usually a good sport, except for the time we decided to make biscuits out of her dusting powders. She chased us around for spankings but never caught up with us. I can still remember racing for the big black phone with a clear plastic dial when it rang. The ring was so loud it would vibrate the phone. There would be five to six people at once on the shared party line.

My Papa was a big man with a countenance like John Wayne. He had a gentle spirit but could intimidate you in a heartbeat. He always drove an old beat-up, red pick-up truck and carried a walking cane he used for many purposes. He poked and prodded the cows, the chickens, the pigs, whatever was in his way. And he loved Listerine. A large bottle always rolled around the dashboard of that old red truck. I can remember the smell of him. He wasn't much on hygiene and his round face always had a shadow of a gray beard. His stubble would graze my face when I hugged him. What teeth he had were half-rotted. He loved to eat, so he carried a large stature and had big jowls. And he wasn't much for health foods, so when I stayed with them, our daily diet would consist of Vienna sausages, a Yoo-Hoo, and a slice of light bread with a bag of candy for dessert.

Before my Mother married Carl, I spent many a day on my Papa's knee. I was the apple of his eye and stuck to his side like glue. He was a tree-cutter by profession, and a known bootlegger in the days of Prohibition. I can still smell the sap and hear the crash of the trees falling as we sat in the middle of the woods in a giant truck. Papa had a crew of five to six muscular black men. They would follow his orders and cut and load the lumber while I was attached to my Papa's back like a Rhesus monkey. I can remember at age two or three, when he would get tired, he'd throw me in the cab of the log-hauling semi, and I would ride in the big round steering wheel. I would climb into the bottom and turn the steering wheel back and forth. Then I'd blow the horn. "Papa, watch me!" And he'd merely chuckle.

On those long days in the woods, we would always leave before dawn and return in the late afternoon. We would ride to the different cutting areas on several tracts of land, ride to the lumberyard and back again, and the whole time Papa would entertain me by singing. He would sing, "You are my sunshine, my only sunshine. You make me happy when skies are gray. You'll never know dear, how much I love you. Oh don't take my sunshine away." To this day, I love the woods, I love the smell of tree sap, and I love to look up and see the rays of sunshine filter through the towering trees and bounce off the ground. Even more, I love the words of that old song from my Papa's deep, cracked voice, a song that takes me to a place of peace and love, a song I sing to my own children today.

I have a poignant memory of smelling tobacco in the small barn on the edge of the road of my grandparents' farm. That sweet smoky smell I'll never forget, and the sight of hundreds of bunches of tobacco leaves hanging upside down, takes me back to that farm. There were always a dozen or so cows roaming the pastures and plenty of pigs; he took great care of his pigs, chickens and goats. I always loved the farm and all the excitement around. Sitting in my Papa's truck in the midst of his simple life is where I always wanted to be. I can still hear him singing our song in his low voice and I can see his comforting smile, which always said, "I love you." I would tell him a hundred and one times, "I love you Papa," and he would always reply, "Papa loves you."

My Papa's downfall was his mismanagement of money. He could always make a dollar but found it difficult to keep one. Maybe it was his generous heart, for he could never say 'no' to his family, friends, or his core crew. He was loyal to them and they to him. There were many Sundays his crew would drive up to Granny and Papa's house to borrow a couple of dollars to feed their kids because they had already gambled or drank their weeks' pay. I can always remember him reaching for his wallet with a short lecture before he handed over the cash.

He tried his hand at farming, but every year he got deeper and deeper in debt due to droughts and high-interest farm loans. He signed his name with an "X" but he knew numbers. Unfortunately, he could never read what he was signing and lost the land on the courthouse steps. My aunt and uncle would later reclaim it by purchasing it out of foreclosure with additional debt. My Mother believed the land had been gifted to them and refused to recognize that there was debt attached, igniting sibling jealousy and a family feud that lasted for years. Carl would continue to use this as a way to poison her mind that her family, her parents, her brother, and her sister, didn't love her. His brainwashing alienated her from her family.

With all my Papa's imperfections, he was still my hero, and I could always make my Papa smile. In his presence, I always felt like his sunshine. I felt a lot of love and a somewhat bit spoiled. He put me on a pedestal and wouldn't dare punish me, even if I deserved it. He died on April 30, 1993, my birthday, within five minutes of the time I was born. The last words he ever spoke to me were, "Pa loves you." Though he had his faults, he was my hero; he gave me an innocent love that I needed so desperately from a male figure. I always knew he loved me, and I knew how very special I was to him. We had a precious bond.

Unbearable Weight

The weight of his body crushed me. I couldn't breathe. I didn't want to breathe. I only wanted him to stop. I just wanted it to be over. I wanted it to stop. It hurt so badly.

Not a word was uttered while he was rubbing me, then he climbed on top of me. I tried to pull away. I squirmed, and he pulled me back to him. "This is for you, because I love you so much. This is our secret." He held my face in his hands and kept stroking my long black hair. "Do you understand how much I love you and want to make you feel good? Do you understand? Look at me! Do you understand?" His sweet, deep tone turned into a low, controlled, growl as he was struggling to complete his task. "If you ever open your mouth and share our secret, you will be sent away. Some people might not understand why you want this so much, and it will hurt your Mother. Do I make myself *g-d* clear?"

He would squeeze my face tighter with one hand until my lips puckered. "Quit sniffling." He began to get angry, and his face turned beet red as the rage rushed to his face. His eyes began to sink back further into his head. Whispering into my ear, "You *g-d* enjoy it. It feels good. You like it." He kissed me hard, sticking his tongue down my mouth as he finished with a loud moan.

He tried to be gentle again, softening his voice, "I did it for you, because you are mine now. I can do whatever I want to you now. I know what's best for you, and I know you like it." He made me look into his eyes, eyes that made my lips quiver with fear. "If you breathe a *g-d* word, not only will you pay, but your bitch Mother will pay, too. You know how I make her pay don't you? You see how I can stomp that *g-d* bitch in the ground, don't you? Do you want to make her pay? Do you want to make her life f------g miserable? You are in control here, and I'll tie your ass in a knot if you even act funny." Then he got off of me. I had heard this many times and didn't doubt a word he said. Sometimes, I wished so hard that he'd do it all in silence, get it over with, and not speak a word. His words hurt every bit as badly as his actions. My heart was pierced with his perversion.

"That hurt worse than what you always do. Can that be the only time you do that to me? Please? That hurt really bad."

"Shut the f--- up, or I'll show you hurt. Go pottie now."

I scooted up to the dinner table only hours later, my feet dangling inches from the floor. Our standard meal lay before me: fried chicken, LeSueur garden peas, rice, gravy, and strong, sweet tea. I ate slowly, barely able to swallow. I couldn't digest the food. Nor could I digest what he had done to me minutes before. It all sat in my throat. My Mother noticed my slow pace of swallowing and asked if I was feeling okay. My mouth opened but nothing came out. Out of the corner of my eye, I saw his fork stabbing my marked arms, stabbing them, and screaming at me to get my *g-d* elbows off the table. I could never put my elbows on the table. It was a rule. I ate quickly, swallowing hard, not knowing what to say or do. A constant stream of tears ran down my face, and then I crawled in bed and went to sleep. He accomplished his mission. I think I was seven or eight, and it became a routine, two to three times a week, some weeks more often than others.

Every day brought more emotional trauma, one more blow to my spirit. I was forbidden to even checkout a book from the library, as he was convinced I needed to read only my textbooks. He would check my book bag as I came through the door and eventually found something he could use to punish me. One day it would be a coloring book and crayons, accusing me of playing at school and not focusing on my studies. He would break my crayons and rip my coloring book to shreds. He would find a stray pencil in my bag and he would call me a thief. I would plead with him that I borrowed it, but he never listened to my pleas, never took my words as valid, and never gave me one opportunity to explain. My words were always slapped away by his open palm across my face.

Tears meant nothing to his cold heart. "I'll give you something to cry about," was his mantra. "I'll give you something to cry about," he would bellow over and over. I would fight back the tears, but it was impossible. Yet, I tried so hard. There was nowhere in the house I could run, never a safe place to hide. My young mind really tried so hard to manipulate my world to control the pain; to lie, to cheat, to steal whatever minutes of peace I could, never knowing when the next bomb would drop, when the next shell would explode. I was such a little girl with such a big problem - he knew how much I feared him, and that the fear would keep me silent.

The Grapevine

I was dragged out of bed on to my butt, awakened from a deep sleep. My head hit the side of the bed and then hit the floor. They were both standing over me screaming. "Why in the hell did you poke holes in this coat?" In my haze of drowsiness, through my sleepy eyes, I saw before me my Mother's long cashmere overcoat with the pretty, chocolate brown fur collar. "You little vindictive bitch," he screamed, "I'll teach you. I'll tie your ass in a knot. I'm going to beat your ass until it bleeds."

"I didn't do it! Please don't hit me. I promise I didn't do it! I swear I didn't!" He turned to my Mother and in a calm manner told her to go about her business; he would take care of me. Calm meant cruel, and I cringed at what was in store for me. He ordered me dressed in five minutes and to meet him outside at the grapevine. I quickly dressed, shaking with every move, and slowly walked to the grapevine, hungry from missing breakfast.

The grapevine was a huge vine built out of iron pipes and clotheslines and covered with huge grape leaves. Spring was on its way. Seasons were changing and most of the leaves were gone. There was a coolness in the air, but being in Mobile, I was in short sleeves. I tried to stay calm, but I was overcome with curiosity. What is he going to do to me? The prominent memories of public humiliation choked me. It was a long walk out the door to the far corner of the backyard where the grapevine grew. His eyes pierced through me. His face showed no mercy.

My shaking intensified as he gave me orders. To my surprise, he had draped a king-sized sheet from the outside of the grapevine. He handed me a stick about a foot long with the diameter about the size of my hand and instructed me to punch holes in the sheet until it was covered with holes. I stopped shaking, even smiled a wee bit on the inside. "I can do this! It will be outside away from his screaming, and I can do this, no problem."

Hours later, with no break for lunch and no bathroom break, I was still punching. I squatted to use the bathroom outside when I could stand it no more. My hands were bleeding from the blisters, and my Mother was begging him to stop. I didn't know if I could keep going. I cried from the pain, and I was so tired, but I worked continuously, and that sheet seemed to grow. With the sun overhead, it was hot and sweat poured off my brow. I was hungry, hot, and tired, but I had to keep going. I had no choice.

I heard the church bells chime in the distance and felt comfort from nowhere. "Jesus loves me this I know, for the Bible tells me so. Little ones to him belong. They are weak, but he is strong." I sang and I punched, and, exhausted and hurting, I finished my task before dark. "Jesus, are you out there? Jesus, do you love me? I'm so scared, and I don't know what to do. Please help me. Please hear me, hear my prayer. I know I'm not a good girl, and I don't know how to be. Please help me be a good girl so You can love me, so You will help me. What happens when no one believes in you, when no one even sees you?"

My hands hurt, my arms ached. I waited for Carl's inspection. I would hold my head down and look at the ground, holding my breath for the next round of cruelty. It had been a hard Saturday. A moth had eaten a hole in my Mother's winter coat, and Carl had eaten a hole through me.

Secret Spills

My babysitter, Mrs. Zimmerman, lived down the street, and I loved going to her house to play. My time there would be brief: in the morning before the bus came, on the weeks his shift work took him in early, and in the afternoons when he was at work, until my Mother could pick me up. Mrs. Zimmerman also kept my baby sister during the days, as needed. The Zimmerman's were a "normal" middle class family who seemed to love each other very much. Mrs. Zimmerman was a heavy-set woman with blue eyes, blonde hair, and a round face with a smile that would light up the room. She was the mother of five girls, so I had to fight for her attention, along with the other group of kids she babysat. She was very sweet, but always going in fifty different directions, and she never took the time to look into my eyes.

From time to time, I would be dropped off at the First Baptist Church of Gulf City, since my Mother would fight for me to go to church. This was the Baptist church in the next town over because the church down the street knew too much. As we could hear the church bells chime from our front yard, I'm sure they could hear God's name taken in vain through the screens of our windows. He never stepped foot inside a church. I can maybe remember one or two Easters. He hated church and cursed everyone there as hypocrites. His morbid jealously would invent men at church interested in my Mother. Today, I'm sure his evil was threatened in the presence of Christ.

Church, like school, became a place in my life for temporary peace, for solace and a brief reprieve from the storm. My very favorite event of the year was Vacation Bible School. Those were the moments I could be a kid and enjoy the simple joys of childhood.

From the perception of the outside world, we were a nice family that lived at the corner of 465 Briar Patch Place. I'm sure they whispered about us behind closed doors. I'm sure they heard Carl's front yard tirades and questioned our isolation. There were neighbors who knew of us and maybe spoke sporadically if we were outside, but no one was allowed inside our world. He made certain I didn't spend time alone with anyone. We were so isolated with our only outside contact coming from TV and family, and he had them all fooled. We had no friends, only people who needed to cross our paths. No one came inside our home. We socialized with no one and went nowhere. There were no social groups, no trips to the movies, and no hobbies, only shopping and working. No one was allowed in our controlled world, *ever*.

Carl had complete control over us; control over what clothes we wore, what and when we ate, and where we went. He even went to the grocery store with my Mother or he went alone, so we would not be seen. Going out to dinner was a rare treat and most of the time it was a trip to a popular Mobile seafood restaurant. Mother and I liked it when he worked was 3 p.m. to 11p.m. shift. Sometimes, we would sneak off and keep our adventure silent. We would ride our bicycles down the street and feel free as birds. All other times I was restricted riding in a small, approximately 30 foot, turn-around adjacent to our home. Round and round I rode until I got so bored that I would just sing and dream. I developed a wonderful imagination that entertained me for hours. It was a privilege to be on my bicycle. I didn't dare complain. The trip around that circle became my carousel of dreams.

I needed those dreams because day after day, I was degraded. "You don't have sense to get out of a shower of s--t," he would bellow as his favorite dig. He would repeat this to me frequently. His other favorite saying was, "you have the brains of a tumble bug," or "you stupid little s--t." I never knew what a tumble bug was until one day, at my Papa's farm, we were looking at the pigs, and he picked up a bug on the pig manure that looked like a beetle and flicked it at me and said, "See, that's a tumble bug." I learned to let Carl's insults roll off me like water. I would draw my mouth tight to my teeth, not a smile, not a frown, a reluctant acceptance of my current state of being.

I learned to transform myself like a chameleon. I learned to adapt, maneuver, manipulate, and alter my feelings to survive. I learned the art of lying, and I could lie without blinking.

"Are you sure this is your Mother's signature on this paper?" Mrs. Butterworth, my third grade teacher, would prod.

"Yes Ma'am, she wasn't feeling well this morning when she signed it, and she scribbled."

"Where is your math test that you made a C on?" she inquired.

Meanwhile, with my magic pen, the C managed to turn into a B, long enough to get a parent's signature, then with white out was returned back to the original

C. I made a mess, and the guillotine dropped. I told Mrs. Butterworth I was going to kill myself if she called my parents. I went home from school that night and ingested a bottle of vitamin A, thinking that would at least make me pass out. Well, it didn't. Mrs. Butterworth brought it to their attention, and they quickly dismissed it as "just looking for more attention." A "problem child" is what I was called. My school career was riddled with discipline problems, as my need to talk and lie kept me in trouble. As much as I chatted in school, my abuse remained secret. Punishments were severe, but I couldn't speak of them. My mischief masked the truth even as the truth drove my mischief, and all my cries for help were ignored.

My memory is void at times. There are things I try to remember, and things I try to forget. Sometimes I welcome the void. Decades later when I return to the little white-brick house where it all happened, the memories explode like grenades all around me. To remember the actions is to remember a time, a place, an event, but to feel them is something so different. When the scars are on the inside, they stay raw. They are bleeding right now, bleeding so heavily the blood from the pain fills my body. I pray that this bleeding is the last; that the writing on these pages is a cathartic end, a release of the past and all the pain it holds. I fear not. I can't believe my Mother still lives in this house. I can't fathom how she has erased from her mind all the memories that saturate these walls. The wind still howls over the worn shingled roof. The walls hold the secrets. They witnessed the injustice. If these walls could talk, they'd only weep. They would weep for the injustice and for all the pain endured within.

I had to get help. I had to tell someone I trusted. Ms. Sams was my young, pretty, fourth-grade teacher with long, blonde hair, and she brought a big smile to school every day. She looked like someone I could trust, someone who would have an answer. I stayed a few minutes after school one day to help her erase the blackboard and wipe off the desks. I blurted it out, "I have been raped." Ms. Sams asked me if I knew what that word meant. I said "no" in a quick lie and waited for the axe to drop, absolutely petrified. She immediately called my parents who marched back to school to explain that I had obviously watched too many soap operas and picked that word up from some adult TV material. Again, my cries for help were dismissed and my tomb of silence sealed tighter. The guillotine fell when I got home and he punished me severely for using the word rape. I resigned never to speak again, because it wasn't worth the consequences. I accepted that this was my life, and I had to figure out how to live in it. At ten, I had so much to figure out. I had big problems and too few tools to cope.

I have learned that the majority of adults don't know how to receive disclosure of sexual abuse. They don't know how to respond, they don't know what to do with the information. Many respond out of fear and denial that leaves children alone to cope. "The disclosure of child sexual abuse disrupts lives; there's no way around that."[2]

CHAPTER 6

The Butterfly

I have a huge pity party for myself on the river, and it feels good. It feels so good to scream, at last to give my pain a voice. It feels good to shake my fist at God and ask, "Why? What did I do to deserve this torture...to deserve my childhood?" It feels good to run to nowhere from nowhere. God has given me time to scream and time to be angry. Finally, I fall to the ground in exhaustion, my face buried in the dirt, defeated. Suddenly, out of nowhere, a lemon-yellow butterfly crouches on my shoulder. It is hard to remain angry with a butterfly staring me in the eye. Then a smile creeps across my face, as I continued to sniffle. I wipe my nose with my sleeve and dry my burning eyes. I sit there for the longest time staring at the butterfly on my shoulder. It seems as though it were trying to comfort me: as if the butterfly is saying to me, "I've been through hell too, but now I'm free." This is exciting stuff for a 32-year-old woman still trembling from childhood nightmares of heinous realities.

Crystal blue skies, white puffy clouds, and cool breezes keep the sweltering heat at bay. The breeze cools the whelps on my face. I try so hard not to think. I try to be still and let go. The butterfly takes flight from my shoulder, and I am sad to see it go away. God has given me a perfectly beautiful day to search for a peaceful place in my soul. I spent such a lifetime in turmoil that rare visits of peace feel foreign. My old friend, fear, seems to lurk at my side. I spent a lifetime wanting what I now find all around me, here for the taking: true peace. I can see it, I can touch it, but I can't seem to hold it. Perhaps it is enough to receive all the beauty around me, to drink in the peace and tranquility and to release my anxiety. God is calling me to do just that. As a child, I had to hold on so tightly to sanity. As an adult, it still terrifies me to let go and receive.

I let the river run through my pain. The taste of fear had digested into bitterness. There was so much anger bottled up inside me, yet I refuse to be an angry person. Therefore, I turned all that anger on myself. I blame me. I believed the lies of the great deceiver. My real father left me, my stepfather abused me, and somehow I was to blame. I must have caused all this pain. This day seemed to release a valve of bitterness stored in the pit of my stomach, bitterness against myself.

I make my way back along the river, feeling some relief. I drive back across the old, rickety iron bridge to the inn, with the sound of the loose metal under my tires. The house is noisy as other guests unpack their cars. I can't stay; I have to be alone. I have to figure out the rest of my afternoon and the rest of my life. I tell myself, "Just try to relax." I can't. Neither my Mother nor Carl ever let me take time to unwind. To this day, this is a discipline where I fail miserably. If I ever rested, I was called lazy.

Back at the bed and breakfast, there is a huge front lawn that borders the river. I lay out my thick, pink and lime green beach towel under the bridge on the shore of the river, by a spot that is very calm. To my right wades a fly fisherman seeking his catch, maybe a speckled trout or a largemouth bass. He is so intent in his cast, so intent on his fly, looking so very peaceful, as his reflection glistens on the water. The river brings him the peace and serenity he seeks. To my left hangs the rusted, red iron bridge with *unwavering strength. I stand in the middle between peace and strength. My heart wants to walk away from the iron bridge and into the peaceful water. I pull out my journal and the sapphire ring. I begin to write.*

Journal Entry June 15, 1997:

Finally, I am alone and at peace with myself for the first time in my life. My mind is perfectly clear, and my focus today is the clean, crisp rushing water, which flows past, echoing a soft lullaby. The rusty, red iron bridge hangs over my head with resolute strength, weathered and worn but towering over the river, waiting for the next traveler to pass over. What a perfect place to cross. There is an army of black ants marching around my towel, ready to attack at any moment. It is so peaceful, so quiet, and yet so noisy with the sound of the water, the sound of the locusts, the whispering of the wind, all the sounds of God, confirming that He's right here with me. The army of ants is in formation and starting its attack. A granddaddy longlegs spider gave me a scare. I feel so very peaceful. Maybe this peace is God. No worries, no woes. I must make this trek an annual event. Never before have I taken time alone, and I really like it. It feels so good to lie here staring at the clouds, guessing their destination. My usual days are spent in a hustle and bustle, hurry up and wait, and then run up and down and side to side. I have perfected the art of busyness. It's another survival technique.

Yet I fear time of reflection will lead to a mental meltdown. If I break again, I don't think I can put myself back together. My head hears the poem: "Humpty Dumpty sat on a wall, Humpty Dumpty had a great fall. All the king's horses and all the king's men couldn't put Humpty together again." Friends tell me, "Life is not a sprint, it's a marathon." If I can ever take time to reflect, to feel the pain, maybe I can figure out how to heal. I live trying not to think about the ugliness, trying to put it out of my mind. If I never thought about it, then it would all go away. My survival strategy has been to cram my days with loads of racing busyness, and then I can wade through my nightmares.

"Dear God, help me to remember these few brief moments of solitude, of contentment, of meditation. Please help me to steal away to these moments in my world at home, if only in my own backyard." I feel a few sprinkles of rain. Of course, it would take a flood to make me move from this spot, to make me leave this moment, a time to recognize that the happiness that has so eluded me is due to the anger and pain from my childhood. It is a moment to forgive myself for the torture I put myself through; a moment to put blame where blame is due.

I try to connect with my emotions. I seek true honesty, for here on the river I am alone and have no reason to lie to myself any more, nor believe the lies Carl spoke over me.

"God please be my Father. Please help me receive your love and healing. You promised in your Word that 'I will be a Father to you, and you shall be my sons and daughters, says the LORD

Almighty.' 2 Corinthians 6:18. Help me to receive you as my true Father. When I look in the mirror, I see so much beauty and so much that is ugly. I look deep into this sapphire ring to find answers, and again, I see so much beauty and so much that is ugly. My life has always been an oxymoron. Help me receive your sapphires, Lord."

Spills of Shame

After the teacher conference with Miss Sams, I couldn't go to sleep. I was so close to telling about the rape, and yet so far. I tested the waters, but I was petrified of full disclosure. My Mother's words to me played over and over in my head. "Why do you want to embarrass me? You know not to use words like that. Rape! I am so ashamed of you. I can't take you anymore! How could you embarrass me like that? I am so ashamed of you!"

Then his words, "Do you want them to take you away to a foster home? Do you want to be placed in a dump of a foster home where you won't be fed, you won't be clothed? Hell, you may not even have a bed to sleep on. Don't lie. It's you. You started it. You want me to touch you. You can't live without it now. You know you like it. You know how good I make you feel. How many times do I have to tell you: this is our secret? Do you understand what a secret means? A secret means it's between you and me. A secret means you never tell another living soul. Do you f----- g understand me? If you open your g-d mouth again, they won't recognize you when I get through with you, g-d it. Do I make myself g-d clear? You keep your g-d mouth shut. You are to never tell. A secret is

77

something you *never* tell." Secret, never tell, secret, never tell, secret, secret, secret.

I climbed into bed. The room was dark, and I hallucinated seeing a python climbing along the ceiling. I clung to the edge of the bed as if it were the edge of life. The walls were paper-thin, and I could hear my Mother and Carl; the moans and groans were unbearable. I put the pillow over my head and tried desperately to smother myself. It was as if an elephant sat on my chest. If I could have pushed a button to leave this world, I would have pounded it as hard as I could with my fist.

The sounds of moans pained my nights and the sounds of screams pained my days. My Mother was so angry and discouraged all the time. She had nowhere to vent her frustration but on me. My Mother would grab me by my long hair and shake me, shake me hard, while screaming out of control. Some days she would bang on my head with her fists. It hurt more than she could ever imagine, but the mental agony was worse than the physical ache. I tried to please her, too, but I couldn't. I despised her as much as I loved her. She didn't protect me, even as I struggled to protect her. She was so very weak, and she took her own torment out on me. She seemed to have no courage to fight back against Cart and risk what teensy bit of security she felt.

Horrendous, demented mind-torture continued. Carl told me for years that I was the reason he hated my Mother. He would tell me all the dreadful things he would do to her if I didn't "shut up, be still" and let him finish. He used the very existence of my Mother to force me to comply. He would throw her against the wall, choke her, kick her, and threaten to kill her and to kill me. He would tell her that if she ever left him, he would kill her. He taught me there was a direct relationship between my compliance and the extent of his cruelty against her. He would threaten to kill her many times, but the emotional and verbal abuse he lashed at her was so much worse.

When someone is ruling over you with an iron fist, screaming constantly about what a worthless g-d person you are, what a whore and a bitch you are, and how simply worthless you are, it beats you down into the dirt. Death, when you are 'living' in the bowels of hell, could be viewed as relief. Compliance was easier to bear than his wrath -- whatever it took to keep him tamed.

I buried my rebellion and my seething hatred against him and learned to manipulate him at every turn. I learned I could exert a tiny amount of control: If I smiled and kept up a good front, I could reduce the severity of his rages. I would anticipate what he needed to keep him calm. I could distract him. I clipped his toenails, I brought him the newspaper, I learned to cook to perfection, spotlessly clean to his specifications, cut the grass on the diagonal, and wash and dry the car, leaving not a single water spot. I worked like a dog, from dawn to dusk, as if the day would never end. I praised Carl, I laughed at his stupid jokes, I tolerated his extreme prejudices against black persons, I agreed with his criticisms of my Mother, I went willingly into the front bedroom, and I let him do as he wished.

Day after day, I learned to maneuver. If he dished out an excessive dose of cruelty, I would just lie there.

He would get mad, but I learned how to play him. I smiled, and he ignored the tears. I learned to smile and cry at the same time. Neither emotion made a difference to him.

He never looked into my eyes. As a matter of fact, no one ever looked into my eyes or they would have seen the suffering, the confusion of a little girl lost in the silence, wandering in the lonely desert of abuse. I tried so desperately to control the hand I was dealt. It was so sad that no one wanted to help or get involved. No one wanted to open the can of snakes. Shame covered me like a wax coating. I felt it every moment of every day. The coating got thicker and thicker with each degrading incident. I kept trying to peel it off, but it was too thick. It would harden and become heavier and heavier with each day he entered me. I've spent a lifetime trying to peel off the tacky wax coating of defilement.

I would hide in the bathroom behind locked doors and scrape my face. I would claw and claw. I would dig my fingernails into my skin. I hated myself. I disgusted myself. I struggled with so many issues, and shame was at the top of the list. He would walk past, rattle the doorknob and scream for me to unlock the g-d door. I had no privacy. He always wanted the door open when I went to the bathroom and when I took a bath; there was never a place to hide. For the next five years, I felt I was in quicksand, sinking into an ever-deepening pit of despair.

From age 10 until 15, I never again attempted to speak the secret. I was intimidated into silence. So I went willingly with him. I complied, sometimes, once a day, sometimes, twice in a day. Then the episodes would play again and again in my sleep. I never escaped the torment, not ever.

Desperate to find my way in my isolation, to deal with the constant threat, I decided to console myself. I became a people pleaser, and tried desperately to be loved by anyone at any cost. At school, I excelled in academics. I tried so hard to click with the good girls, then the bad, then the rejects. Never finding a clique of my own, I bounced from friend to friend. Pain and rejection became my constant companions.

I was considered a strange bird. I created a false self, a false identity that had no true north, no constant. I began to feed my self-hatred. I was criticized for breathing, as it was never right. With that kind of day in and day out berating, I began to punish myself. I would replay all the negatives I heard in a day. I continued to spiral down into a very dark place with a distorted view of myself and of others. I never knew what normal was or what happiness felt like. Never connecting with my true feelings on the inside, I would be what anyone wanted me to be. I could cut them to pieces with my thoughts of resentment and jealously. People became objects of my anger. I had nowhere to vent, no place to scream. I screamed inside, and unfortunately, I screamed at myself.

Leanne was cute, smart, and the most popular girl in my class. Her nearly perfect family kept her in every activity, every church function, and every school play. She played the piano at church and baseball at the ball field around the corner from my house. The field was so close I could hear the cheers, yet never was I allowed to participate in the games.

Leanne's parents were sweet people. I hated Leanne for her normal life. I hated her for her popularity. I hated her for her innocence. She had everything I wanted, even her friendship. She was all "it" and I felt like I was nothing.

CHAPTER 7

Growing in Pain

My body was changing through puberty, and he liked it. The pain in my chest hurt something awful; I would grimace when he groped me. The curse of Eve visited me quite early. It frightened me, as I had no preparation for what was happening to me, certainly no mother-daughter talks. My Mother simply handed me a tampon at age ten and said, "Use this." I didn't know how to "use this." It was a day or two before I figured out you discard the cardboard. When he had me alone, he whispered that I could get pregnant now and that "we" would have to be careful.

My periods were dreadful, with stomach cramping and heavy bleeding for days. He had no clemency, no sympathy. Mother accused me of using it to get attention. She gave me no comfort, but she did give me a cold adolescent talk. The talk about the birds and the bees consisted of, "If you do 'the thing,' you can get pregnant now. Never do 'the thing' with anybody. 'The thing' is very bad." I remember staring at her, wanting so desperately to say, "You mean 'the thing' your husband has been doing to me for years?"

Each room in the palace at 465 Briar Patch Place was painted. The middle bedroom, as it was called, was yellow, the guest bedroom, his place of twisted lust, was pink, and their master bedroom was blue. Every bedroom was exquisitely decorated with custom-made draperies, quilted silk bedspreads, velvet pillows piled high, and matching ornate bedroom furniture. All the bedrooms had king-size beds with huge, wooden carved headboards. All the beds were made for kings. It was a rare weekend when my Granny came to visit for a few days. Carl was usually on his best behavior in front of the outside world, but not today. I woke up in my bed in a puddle of blood, in the middle bedroom I shared with my baby sister. During my menstrual cycle, I usually got up all during the night to make sure I didn't bleed on the mattress. We had a new mattress, and he screamed at me regularly, daring me to ruin his mattress.

This particular night, I guess because I felt safe with my Granny under our roof, I slept hard and didn't get up during the night. When I awoke, I ran to the bathroom to try and get cleaned up, but he spotted the mess before I could return. He hit me with his fist so hard that my head spun, and he shrieked that I just wanted attention and wanted everyone to know. He then snatched off his belt and flailed it as hard as he could. My Granny bawled and begged him to stop hitting me, saying that she would clean it up. "You animal, stop hitting her! She can't help her cycle," she begged. He ignored her. That day my Granny got a glimpse into my hell ... but she did nothing.

It was a Saturday, and everyday chores crowded our agenda. He was at work on the evening shift and had given us the garage as the first item on the list, and my Mother was attempting to help. I knew where he kept his stash of condoms (rubbers, as we knew them), since he would make me go get them from time to time whenever he summoned. To the right of the kitchen door in the garage sat an old wooden stereo console that she was about to move, and they were behind the stereo inside the cabinet casing. Now was my big chance to reveal the secret without using any words. It could be by accident that she discovered them. He wouldn't kill me if she discovered them accidentally. When she moved the stereo, there was a chance they would fall out, especially if I tipped it backwards. This old stereo kept me company many afternoons when I could listen to "Mr. Postman" or "Oh Let Me Be Your Teddy Bear." At the time, it was my salvation.

My heart was beating so fast my palms sweated. In two seconds, my secret would be out. She would see the teal green Trojan box and know they weren't used with her because she had an IUD. The sound of the wood scraping the concrete brought me out of my daze, and I grabbed the other side, "Let me help you." I pushed it back and tilted it, and out they dropped. We both eyed them at the same time. I must have turned white as a sheet. Not a word was uttered. She picked up the box, threw it into the huge, black plastic garbage bag, and went about her cleaning. There was no emotion, no questions, no reaction, and no opportunity for me to respond. She never asked, "What is this?" or "Where did these come from?" or "Who put them here?" If her mind was pondering the green box, her reaction was buried in denial. There wasn't even a hint of speculation. I stood stunned.

All my hopes lay paralyzed on my tongue. I was ready to spill the beans. I wanted to throw-up. I wanted to run so fast and so far, but I couldn't leave this garage because it had to be spotless by 3:15 p.m. when he returned from work. Why couldn't I tell her?

Was I absolutely gutless, or did the thoughts of the horror of it all sound in my head so loud that I lacked the courage to speak up? What would telling the secret do to her and to others in our family? Somehow, I felt I ruined her first marriage. They might have had a chance to make it work had there not been a baby on the way. I had to put my baby sister first now.

At eleven, I could change diapers and bottle-feed the baby, and my Mother never denied the help. This was work I loved. Taking care of my baby sister gave me a purpose and took my mind away from my revulsion. I desperately wanted out of this sick mess. The trap was unbearable and unbreakable.

One Sick Day

The deed was done. The vomit was charging toward my throat. My body was covered in sweat, but I couldn't move. He had fallen asleep with his leg over me, and his breathing was heavy and laborious. I didn't dare wake him for fear of the monster that would surface and the vile utterances that would heave from his mouth. He might start again, and I couldn't bear another round. I tried to inch my body out of his bondage. I tried not to breathe. "God, please let me get up. Please make him turn over without waking." Lying there in misery, I prayed. "God, if you're out there, please help me. Please let me get up. I feel so sick." I was washed in sweat, and my blood boiled from fever.

I was vomiting on and off all night and reluctantly stayed home from school. I was sick with the flu, and I was so stupid to think he would leave me alone. I was so sick, but it didn't matter, and now I desperately needed to slip out of this bondage to go throw up. He had worked the night shift and was dead with exhaustion, wanting me only to lie with him. He said he would sleep, but no, the monster wanted his pleasure before his sleep, and now I was trapped beneath his limbs, begging God for escape.

My face was crunched under his face, and each breath would cover me like a fog, the smell of his sulfur breath nauseating me. He was snoring loudly and deep asleep. He turned, and I was released. I slithered out of bed, straight to the toilet where I hung my head and sought to vomit the vile scum within me. I wanted to vomit out the feeling of him inside me. The frayed, picked-mauve washcloth with bleach spots would not wash away his fingerprints, no matter how hard I scrubbed. I could not wash the shame off, inside or out.

At this time in my life, I could barely look at myself in a mirror. The mirror only reflected shame, more shame than a young girl could bear. I ached for a taste of innocence, not shame. I cupped my hands for water under the bathroom sink faucet. My head hurt, and my knees went weak. My mind would race to a disease fantasy. I thought, "Maybe I have a dreadful disease, and I can die soon." I wanted to die, so much more than I wanted to live. Yes, death seemed like a dream, a peaceful dream.

I stumbled to the couch - the forbidden couch that we couldn't sit on – tip toeing so as not to wake the sleeping giant. I was too strong to die and too weak to live. I existed somewhere in between. The only comfort I had was a scripture I had heard at church the past Sunday, from 2 Corinthians 12:9, "My grace is sufficient for you, for my power is made perfect in weakness. Therefore I will boast all the more gladly about my weaknesses, so that Christ's power may rest on me." I needed Christ's power to rest on me.

Denial and Detachment

He went to elaborate lengths to hide our time behind closed doors from everyone – even abusing me while my younger sisters were in the house. As they sat zoned in front of the TV, he sent me outside to wash the car. Then I was to sneak through the living room after the outside kitchen door slammed. Yes, I walked through the throne room, the living room, to the front bedroom, the guest bedroom where the spread would be neatly pulled back from the foot of the bed and folded over twice. Yes, I walked. I wasn't dragged. I walked into his web. I knew how she would suffer if I didn't go willingly. I participated. The awful soup of his smells, the sulfur from the plastics plant, Brut Cologne, Efferdent and Vitalis hair grease, all combined gagged me. The strong smells along with the taste of fear and repulsion made me nauseated.

I left my body. I decided he could not control my thoughts, and I would not think of him or what he was doing to me. Mentally, I took myself to a place where I could cope. I went to the ocean. I heard the waves, not his words. I felt the sand on my feet and the sun on my body and not his hands. He disgusted me. I would tell myself it would be over soon. "A few more minutes and it will be over. Hang in there, just a few more minutes. Stay at the beach, just focus, find a sand dollar with your toes, dig deeper into the sand. Taste the salt water on your lips, feel the sun on your face."

He was sickeningly careful: the bedspread would be turned neatly back down, as all beds in the tiny palace were always made. I couldn't do my homework or relax, because it was time for dinner, and my Mother would be home from college soon and expect dinner on the table. She was working on her master's degree and went straight from work to class. I quickly began to fry the pork chops and open our staple LeSueur garden peas and put the rice on to cook. He lay on the couch and watched TV while I worked. She came home tired and in a most foul mood, as usual. The pork chops were burning, and he was yelling at me, "Can't you do a *g-d* thing right? You are so *g-d* stupid, you *g-d* ignorant little bitch, you've burnt our *g-d* dinner!" I needed to go to the bathroom so I could claw my face, so I could peel off the disgrace, the shame. I became resistant to the pain outside, but buried it deep inside where it burned constantly.

I got an infection, a nasty infection, "down there," and I tried to tell her. Of course, she told him, and he accused me of "doing the deed with the S.O.B. next door." "You *g-d* whore, you bitch of a whore, you are f-----g every punk boy that wears pants, you even smell like a whore," he screamed as he stripped off his belt and lashed it at me. My Mother chimed in, "I told you not to do 'the thing.'" Then, I could never tell her anything else. With either of them, every time I opened my mouth, I paid a price.

She read my diary. She said she wanted to know what made me "tick," since she didn't really "know me." She got more "tick" than she bargained for. She stoically closed it. What lay inside never crossed her lips. She was burying herself deeper and deeper into the denial. She said, "I am doing the very best I can for you." To this day, she repeats, "I did the best I could."

As adolescent years rolled into teens, I began to beg him to stop. I bargained to no avail, and he shrewdly blackmailed me with freedoms that a teen desperately desires. I got to go to a football game if I didn't put up a fight that day. He tortured me all day, and he kept adding to the ante. I wanted to go so bad I would have walked though fire naked. He made me use my mouth, and that's what got me to the football game.

I started putting up a fight. I threatened to tell all. He pulled a gun, a silver-barreled, pearl-handled pistol, from under the lip of the towering armoire in his room. We struggled, and he put the pistol barrel in my mouth and said, "I don't think you will." It scraped the roof of my mouth, and all I could do was shake. He called me a "g-d whore, a g-d bitch, a nothing that nobody will ever want." He pried me open; he had his way. He felt his control slipping. He scared me worse than ever that day.

I had to get out. I had to outsmart him. I had to make a plan, one that I could have in place, fill my Mother in on and execute. She was so scared that she wouldn't be able to take care of us, and he kept repeating his threats of killing her. She could not hold a job for long. He robbed her of her self-confidence and kept her on the cusp of a nervous breakdown. He was all about the money, and it was not acceptable for her not to work. I started thinking about my plan night and day. I thought of all the different ways I could kill him. I reasoned that we could survive financially with his life insurance benefits. I thought of poisoning his food.

When he worked the night shift, I had his dinner cooked and on the table when he arrived home at 11:15 p.m. School night or not, my Mother would go to bed, and I was expected to stay up and prepare a hot meal for him. I hated this time. He would grope me in the open. He was getting braver and braver, as if he didn't care if she found out, as if he didn't care if she walked in on us, as if he knew she knew already. My plan would be perfect. Plan A: I would poison his food, and no one else would accidentally eat it. This could work.

Plan B: He was under the car working. It was jacked up, and I had to hold the handle. The adrenalin ran through my veins. I could kick the jack out from under the car, and hopefully he would die instantly. It would all be a tragic accident. I wouldn't rot in prison. It would all be innocent enough. No one would suspect. But I stood motionless. I had no guts. In the dark of the night, I plotted other ways for him to die and other ways out of this mess.

I had learned my real father lived in Danbury. I thought I might escape to his house. I knew our high school cheerleading squad was going to Danbury for a summer camp. Could I possibly make the cheerleading squad? I had been to one ball game. I saw what they did. I watched them practice in the gym during physical education classes. What was I thinking? How would I ever get Carl to let me try out? This was a big, big dilemma. I started begging. Every minute of every day, I begged. I cut the grass without complaint, I cooked, washed the dishes, washed and dried the laundry, and then I begged some more. I was already the maid, the cook, the nanny, the yard boy, and the car washer.

My Mother pursued her master's degree, and that kept her out of the house and out of his line of fire. As I was left to perform her domestic duties, I became determined to find my *real* father. I went to Carl and begged: "Please, please, please; I'll go willingly with you. I won't complain, just please let me try out for cheerleading. I'll keep up with my chores and I'll make straight A's. Please let me do it!" Miracles do happen; he consented.

There was a second miracle. I couldn't turn a cartwheel, but I made the Mobile Christian Junior Varsity cheerleading squad. (Instead of "angels in the outfield," for me they were in the gym.) Phase I, mission accomplished. Every practice, every game, every cheer was a battle. Cheerleading forced me into a new arena, and I was not prepared for it. It made me popular overnight, and I had more friends "than I could shake a stick at". I loved it, and, looking back, I consider this year the best of my youth.

First 'Love'

I met my first puppy love on the football field. Jay was the yearbook photographer, and I noticed him taking pictures of me at the game and at the pep rallies and then around school when I wasn't even in my cheerleading uniform. He admired me from afar, and I felt his lens on me at all times. When I visited the darkroom with him, he showed me the "wall of Angela" covered with photos of me. Through cheerleading, I found freedom, I found friends, and I found love. I kept the monster satisfied to get to Phase II of my plan.

CHAPTER 8

Face to Face

World War II was nothing compared to the conflict that took place over my headstrong determination to go to this cheerleading camp in Danbury. I aimed to find my real father and look him in the eye at any cost. I was 15, and I had won the battle (if not the war) to pack my bags for a weeklong camp. I was elated. Free from the verbal abuse for a week, free from the sexual abuse for a week, free from physical abuse for a week, free from the arduous chores, free from having to fake acting happy. I had a smile glued on my face that would have won the national cheerleading competition without one leap, jump, cartwheel, or routine. I had a mission: it was to have a great time with my friends, to locate my real father and devise a creative escape plan.

The first day opened my eyes to a great college campus and lots of giggly girls. They kept us extremely busy learning routines and techniques. The second day I was desperate to make my move. I told my friend, Samantha, that I needed to sneak out of the dorm where we were sleeping that night, and she had to cover for me. I told her I'd only be gone an hour or two. She didn't like the idea at all, as her world would end if she got kicked off the cheerleading squad. These girls did not have a clue. They all lived in "la la land," worried about their hair, their acne, and their big egos. It was the Southern equivalent of a "valley girl" convention, and I was there by destiny. I told her I had never seen my real father, and he lived in this very town, very close to campus. I told her she had no choice but to help me, because this was my only chance, and I couldn't go back to Mobile without having seen him. I had waited 15 years to lay eyes on him, and this was the night. This was my only chance, and I was here for this moment, for this reason. She looked outside herself and agreed to cover for me. While she feared the consequences of acting as an accomplice, I feared the night that lay ahead.

We developed a plan. We stuffed my bed with pillows, and Samantha told the chaperone that I wasn't feeling well and went to bed early, which she believed, since I had asked for two aspirin after dinner. Samantha covered well for me, and I was indebted to her always. We had no phones in the dorm, and I could not get caught in the lobby searching for a phone and a phone book. I had to be smart. I had watched enough James Bond movies to pull this off. I peered around each corner and slipped out an exit door on the ground floor of the dorm. I walked to the nearest payphone at a station on the corner. I turned up the phone book that hung on the metal chain, licked my fingers and thumbed to the Ws.

I quickly found Wells. I knew his first name was Norbert, and very quickly found a possible listing – N. G. Wells, 743 Laurel Lane. My stomach leaped into my throat. I had his number in my hands, and all I had to do was dial. I took a deep breath, put my dime in the pay phone, and dialed the number very slowly. I waited, and the loud rolling ring began to echo in my ear. One, two, and a "Hello." I panicked and hung up.

I had not even rehearsed what I was going to say. I began to beat myself up. "Stupid, stupid, stupid. Just ask to speak to Norbert and say you are Angela.

He'll know your name. He'll be thrilled to hear your voice. Come on, Angela, you can do this. Just dial." I dug another dime out of my pocket, and I couldn't waste this one because I didn't have very much money. I think my parents gave me ten dollars for the week, and I had already spent half of that on junk. "Please God, make it be okay. Let him know who I am and make him want to see me. Please." I dialed again and this time the phone only rang once before a male answered again.

"Can I speak to Norbert?" I could barely say as my voice quivered.

"This is Bert. Who is this?" the voice blared back, almost annoyed.

Shyly I said, "My name is Angela, and I'm your daughter." There was a long silence, an unbearably long silence. I broke the silence with a stream of conversation. I wouldn't allow rejection. I had come too far. "I'm at Alabama Southern College and wanted to see if we could meet. I've been really curious my whole life at what you look like. Can you come pick me up from the 7-Eleven down the street from the college?"

He hesitated and then responded, "So you're in college." My ears began to burn, and I realized he didn't even know how old I was. I began to get so angry that he probably hadn't thought about me since he walked away from me fifteen years before. My mind flooded with insecurities.

"No, I'm here at a cheerleading camp for my high school. Do you want to see me or not?" I continued as the tears began to flow down my cheeks.

"Yes, I'll see you. I'll be there in ten minutes," he responded abruptly and hung up the phone.

The next ten minutes seemed like an eternity. I stood there in the dark, scared to death, scared of the unknown. I looked up at the stars and prayed. "God, please let this be my ticket out. Please make him love me the way a daddy is supposed to love his little girl. Please make him love me." The most uncomfortable hour of my life lay ahead.

Shortly, an old, dented blue Chevy came into view, turned into the 7-Eleven parking lot, and drove right up to the pay phone. The driver was a middle-aged, heavy-set woman with a disheveled appearance. She looked back at me and grinned. It was a grin that made me so uncomfortable, as if she knew something I didn't. The passenger door opened and out stepped the biggest nerd I had ever seen. My stomach sank as he opened the back door of this dirty, trashed, blue Chevy. There was no physical contact. No smile, no pat on the back. Without a word, he opened the door, and I quietly climbed in. I slid into the backseat thinking to myself, "I was just kidding. I'll stick to my fantasy of you."

He turned around in the seat and started the third degree, peering over his black-rimmed glasses: "How old are you? What grade are you in? Where do you live? What is your favorite subject?" He would squeeze his eyes and flair his nostrils. "Do you make straight A's?" And the ridiculous questions went on and on. As I answered the nonsense, I was examining the man. I was so disappointed. He had hair crawling out of his nose and longer ones crawling out of his ears. He had greasy, black hair with a huge dose of dandruff and eczema all around his face. His big, round stomach matched his big round face that was as cold as ice. He had not one twinkle of love in his eyes. For him, this evidently was all a formality, one that he was expecting at some point in his life. He had no remorse, no shame, and no connection.

The balance of the conversation centered on him and what a magnificent person he was. He had two doctoral degrees and had won the top salesman awards for selling vacuums and encyclopedias. He was very full of himself, going on and on about how great he was in every way. The words turned into "blah, blah, blah, blah."

"If you are the least bit intelligent, you got that from me." His inferiority complex shown like the Northern Star, and my Northern Star he was not. He was the know-it-all of know-it-alls.

We arrived at a nice, red-brick ranch home. It was exactly as my Mother had described. It looked massive from the outside, and I remember thinking, "They are rich." I was taught to equate wealth by the size of someone's home and the car they drove. I've since learned better. As we entered through the screen door, he explained that it was his parents' house, where he and his family also lived.

Within seconds, I met a feeble, gray-haired old man who was short and stocky and dressed in cream-colored coveralls. He introduced himself as N.G. Wells, my grandfather, and behind him stood a stoic, older woman with a drawn up mouth, my grandmother, who could only say, "Darling, we've wanted to find you for years," … as if I had been lost.

I had hoped this would be a nice place to land. My hopes were dashed. It was all so overwhelming, that I became dizzy. The house stunk of stale smoke smells, as if a window had never been opened to allow fresh air in. It was cluttered from corner to corner with junk: books, magazines, bags, clothes, boxes, and clutter. They wanted me to sit down, and I respectfully asked if I could use their restroom first.

In the bathroom mirror, I quickly caught my reflection in the spotted mirror, and looked down at the cluttered vanity and kept shaking my head in disgust. I wanted to get out of there immediately. My plan had not been laid beyond the phone call.

They sat me in a chair in the living room, as if I were on display, and continued the inquisition. I wouldn't want to spend one day with these people, so I quickly decided to tell them anything they wanted to hear and get back to the dorm. I continued the pleasantries and explained that I had sneaked out of the dorm and really could only stay a few minutes. I told them I wanted to say "Hi" and that maybe we could write every once in a while. I shared a glimpse of my picture-perfect life, telling them I had two sisters, I played the piano, loved the beach, my Mother was a schoolteacher and doing fine. I told them my father worked at the plastics plant, and I made straight A's at Mobile Christian School and was a cheerleader.

They questioned me about my Mom's family, my Aunt Hazel, Uncle Ted, and my grandparents, and I filled them in briefly on their lives. They laughed when I told them my Papa had nine lives, because he had lived through two train wrecks. I told them my parents would have a cow if they knew I was here and that my father was very strict. We agreed to secrecy, that we did not want to upset my parents, and we could correspond from time to time through my aunt. (This became just one more secret I had to manage.)

I could tell they weren't really interested in getting involved in my world. They spent the rest of the time telling me about their family farm and their motor home and their travels. My grandmother recounted her career as a librarian at the local college, and my grandfather's claim to fame as assistant postmaster in the hamlet. She leaned over and asked me point blank, "Do you know Jesus, Darlin'?"

I answered in puzzlement, "Yes ma'am, I was born again at age twelve." She immediately went into a long dissertation about how they loved Jim and Tammy Faye Baker, faithfully gave to their ministry and had taped every episode of the PTL Club. I could believe it, looking at all the videotapes around the room. Norbert sat silently, glaring at me. His wife smiled and kept telling me how pretty I was. My grandfather sat reclined in his Lay-Z-Boy, smoking one cigarette after another. He said he had a back injury and had to take some pills to ease the pain and spent most days in his recliner.

I listened to my grandmother talk about Uncle Theodore, who died in a plane crash while crop dusting, Uncle Brice, Aunt Jude and Uncle Bob, and Aunt Ada and this cousin and that cousin. By now, my eyes had glazed over, as this was all a bit overwhelming. All the while, I was having a dialogue in my mind, thinking, "This entire bunch of people can't help me get out of a paper bag, much less the mess I'm in."

I snapped to and started to plead, "I'm sorry, but I really need to get back now before I get into a lot of trouble." I stood up and Norbert wanted to hug me. It was the coldest hug I had ever received, as if I was hugging a glacier in Alaska, and I made it as brief as possible. No words were spoken between us. When he thrust his body at me, I wanted to puke. My grandparents didn't know how to say goodbye. They stood up and tried to follow Norbert's lead. It was all so awkward, but I tried to be as gracious as possible, thanking them for having me and promising to write soon.

The five-minute ride back to the dorm was silent, and you could have cut the air with a knife. I got out and said "thank you." So it was that my real father, whom I had just met less than an hour ago, waved goodbye, and drove away leaving me alone in the dark. I forced my legs to walk back into the dorm. There is no adjective in the English language to express how crushed my heart felt, no way to communicate how it feels when the person that gave me life rejected me. The single dash of hope for deliverance from my abuse was extinguished by his cold indifference.

My steps were heavy with disillusionment. I was drowning in cynicism. I slithered down the hall and made it back to my bed safe and sound. My roommates wanted all the details, and I told them I couldn't talk about it tonight. "Please, let me be." The tears puddled on my pillow, and I felt the soaking wet cloth clenched to my face. I cried most of the night with my face buried, hoping I'd suffocate before morning.

I faced the next day with piercing doom. I had to continue the motions as we worked hard from dawn till dusk in the one-hundred-degree July heat, and my strength was waning. I had to refocus and remember why I was here: to win the cheerleading squad championship for the Southeast and not to find my real father and my deliverance from my hell on earth. Though I was crushed, the show must go on.

Desertion's Wounds

Through the years, I have realized another attack on my soul -- the one from my biological father. He left me. He consciously chose to abandon his own child. That was a fact. But why? That question has twist-tied my emotional cells. His abandonment left a gaping hole in my heart. It made me feel like I didn't mean enough as a person for him to love me. I figured I didn't count for anything in his eyes, except to walk away. That feeling bled into my life every day and into every relationship. I felt as if I had to do everything possible to keep every relationship close, so my inner circle of support would stay strong. When you are abandoned, your sense of security vanishes. Even now, I hold so tight, with my fingertips, not my fists, so it won't hurt so badly if someone I love walks away.

Like Father, Like God?

For way too long, I looked to God as I had looked to my biological father and my stepfather. I worried that God would desert me, and I feared God as I did my stepfather. It took me a long time to learn the true character of God. It took me longer still to accept the true love of God, which in no way resembled the love of my father and my stepfather. I had no roots, no stake in the ground to cling to which said: "I know who I am, and I know my purpose." Until I came to know Christ and let Him have control of my life, I did not value me. Abandonment and sexual abuse stole my identity, and Christ gave it back. These twin torments erased my self-worth, and Christ wrote it new, fresh, and strong. It has taken a lifetime to discover who I am in Christ and who Christ is in me.

CHAPTER 9

The Resilient Rebel

Carl had decided that he wanted to be a cattle farmer, and I spent many days in the fields on my Granny and Papa's farm with him planting rye and millet to feed the cows. I gained physical strength loading 100-pound bags of fertilizer and seeds. The heat in the fields would be so intense that the lime from the fertilizer would melt on my hands and burn them on the spot. My hands would blaze like fire, and I would forget and wipe the sweat from my brow before it dropped into my eyes. Stupidly, I would then wipe the fertilizer into my eyes. The blazing sun seared my every move while Carl cracked the whip.

There were days on end where I would pull barbed wire fences through the brush and the creek. Sweat would drip from my chin as I crawled through the muddy creek, sinking in sludge. This was another hidden place where he would force his pleasure.

My old friend fear was always close by, always hovering over me, ready to take advantage in the isolation. We would come in from the fields to eat dinner at my Granny's house, and she would rant and rave that I was too young to endure the heat, especially without a hat. She had no idea what I was forced to endure. I prayed that they were all ignorant and not negligent. I prayed they cared and didn't think, didn't know, didn't want to know. I came into her home wanting only a hug and a few minutes of peace from her, a few words of encouragement from her; these always welcomed me. She always encouraged me to keep looking up and to get my education. "Git your degree 'cuz no one can ever take away your education," she would say. "You are going to make it one day, you are going to make it with wings." I always loved that saying. It echoes through my mind to this day: "Make it with wings."

Years later, I asked her why no one did anything about the abuse. "Why did everyone look the other way? Why?" She denied ever seeing it. I really think it was too horrible a sin for anyone to face. Today sexual abuse surrounds us, and no one chooses to see it. Everyone looks the other way.

They too feared Carl and, as sick as it sounds, by paying rent on their land for his cows, he effectively purchased their silence. It may not have been his master plan, but it certainly worked. They were starved for the next dollar, and he fed them. I blamed everyone in my life. Ignorance is no reprieve in my book. And yet, I knew there was a cycle of dysfunction; if my Mother had felt loved as a child, then she would not have been so desperate to marry just anybody, and ended up marrying the devil. She might have been happy and found a soul mate to create a loving home. That was what she wanted. It is so clear to me now how truly sad it is that the sins of the parents are passed down to the children. Their faults are reflected in the lives of their heirs. She claims my grandparents didn't love her enough, and therefore she couldn't love herself. Maybe she ignored my abuse to prevent facing her own. I refused to perpetuate this cycle of destruction, and I vowed that one day I would break the cycle, that one day I would succeed. I made a conscious choice.

My physical strength fed my mental strength. I had no room for weakness in my life. I had no time to belabor my failed attempt at escape. I quickly surmised I had to either get a job or get married. At sixteen, it should be easy to get a job, so I set out to do that. I pursued a man to marry as plan B, and plan C consisted of prayer like I've never prayed before. My ritual birthday wish became a daily prayer chant. I prayed for a happy family. "God, please fix this family. Please make him stop." I fantasized that I would tell my Mother and together we would go to therapy. He would stop the outrage against us and the small bouts of fun would expand daily. We would eliminate his rampages, and the abuse would cease. Carl would have a lobotomy, beg forgiveness and become a Godly man. My Mother would understand and emerge from her sea of depression and take her rightful place as my Mother. She would love me, and we as a family would play, laugh, and listen to one another. Our home would be filled with joy and our voices would be soft and encouraging. We would smile, and I could look in the mirror and like the person looking back at me. I wanted what I saw on the TV screen. I wanted a family like "Little House on the Prairie," "The Brady Bunch," and "The Waltons." I snapped quickly back into reality, and my daydream drifted a million miles away. I was so far from those fantasies that every day I became less of a person, and every day I became more and more confused. I yearned for peace and harmony, for my virtue restored, and a day to laugh.

Sources of Salvation

I had accepted the Lord Jesus at the age of twelve. The song that the congregation sang said, "I serve a risen savior, He's in the world today, and I know that He is living, no matter what men may say. I hear His voice of mercy and you ask me how I know He lives, He lives within my heart." That day at church, I hung on every word the pastor spoke. "If you want to be saved, all you have to do is ask Jesus into your heart. He will heal your pain, and He will deliver you today."

Sign me up, I thought. I want to be saved, I'm in a lot of pain and I need to be delivered, because I can't figure a way out on my own. I ran forward when the invitation was given as my Mother pulled at my dress asking me if I was old enough to make this decision. I struggled to get loose and continued through the pew to the front. It was brief as the pastor prayed the sinners' prayer with his hand on my head. He told my Mother I'd be baptized the next Sunday. He finished by telling me that I had been born again today. The next Sunday, he told me my sins had been washed away, and I was a new creation in Christ. I do remember a change in me. The "*g-d's*" cut worse than usual. I wanted to read my Bible, and I prayed without ceasing. I stayed on this path for about three months, until I became so disillusioned. I wanted answered prayer, and I wanted it right then. I didn't merely want answers, I was desperate, and I wanted God to know just how desperate I was. I pleaded for answers.

I came home from my salvation experience only to be thrust back into the bowels of hell. I was deeply confused because I did not feel pure. I expected to feel clean; I expected powerful change in my home life. I expected answer to prayer. None of that occurred. It seemed to me that sin chose me; I didn't choose it. To make matters worse, I couldn't make my body *not* participate. I couldn't control the primal response to his touch. Do I even go deeper to describe how horrific this experience was and how perverted I felt? It filled me with shame. Shame boiled up inside me. I hated him, I hated me, and I hated what he did to me. How could I enjoy any of this? How was I going to make it through another day?

I couldn't look in the mirror. I began to paint my face with as much make-up as I could cake on. I felt like trash, pure white trash. There was no place I could look inside that made me feel good, not a crevice. I couldn't look into the mirror, I couldn't look into my Mother's face, and I couldn't look up to God. I could only hang my head in despair. If I could have crawled under a rock and died, I would have done so gladly. Somehow, something kept me dredging onward, something deep inside that I wanted to identify.

How could God love me? I was scared of God, terrified of Him, just as I was terrified of Carl. I didn't resemble any other Christian at First Baptist Church of Gulf City. It seemed to me they all had perfect lives and could easily follow God. I couldn't even get through twenty-four hours without hearing God's name taken in vain. I kept hearing that I was a child of God, fully accepted by His grace, covered in His mercy. How could I be someone God would want in His family? I lived on the dark side and in a dark place. The light I felt from God was blinding. The people at church were distant. At twelve, I couldn't shave my legs, and that doesn't sound too bad, but I couldn't wear panty hose either, so at age twelve, I was dressed in little-girl dresses with tight collars and forced to wear frilly ankle socks. I was so not-cool. I got sneers and laughs from the other girls in my Sunday school class. It didn't feel good to be there, and it didn't feel good to listen to the sneers and giggles every time I entered the room. They made fun of the way I dressed, the way I walked, the way they heard Carl curse at me in the front yard, the fact that I could never go anywhere, anytime. It was all very funny to them and all very hurtful to me.

The days wore on, and my search for a way out was futile. I manipulated a few dates with Jay. We had so much fun together. I was another person when I was with him. He pursued me and fell head over heels in love with me, or maybe he fell for the challenge, for the mystery. Walks on the beach, heated make-out sessions, and trips to the dark room to develop the yearbook pictures made for a sweet romance, a short diversion from my misery. Our puppy love ended the night he took our relationship to the next level; he knew I was messed up. I freaked out when his hands roamed over my body. He, too, only wanted to use my body for his pleasure. He spoiled the innocence of our relationship. "Just take me home!" I screamed at him. "Just take me home, and don't ever look my way again!" He thought he had Sybil in the back seat of the car. The poor guy didn't have a clue how emotionally depleted I was.

I was upset for weeks after the incident. I alienated him. Even though I missed him desperately, we continued to play cat and mouse over the next year. He knew I had issues, and I knew he was a teenage boy with no commitment and a lot of mojo. I only wanted to be loved. I missed the attention he gave me. He made me feel special, and the time I spent with him made me forget my troubles. He was an exit strategy. I begged him back, willing to pay any price for his attention.

Meanwhile, I did everything in my power to alleviate Carl's tirades in our home, and sometimes, though rarely, I succeeded. The age of sixteen definitely came with advantages, one of which was driving cars. We owned an older Camaro, a three-year-old Grand Prix, and a new Buick Regal. Carl would take the Camaro to work because the pollution released at the plastics plant might damage the brand new car. To him, things were always so much more important than people were.

One morning, Carl was on the first shift, 6 a.m. to 3 p.m., and he left for work early. We were all running late as usual, and the new car was parked in its customary spot, the tiny, one-car garage. In my haste, I tore out of the garage and accidentally took down the hinge of the garage and scraped the entire fender of the brand new Buick. My Mother freaked and started to scream at me, which was her normal response in a crisis. We were all late, so I convinced her to let me skip school, and I promised to get it all fixed by 3 p.m., when Carl would be headed home. She reluctantly agreed and called the school to let them know I would be absent. With a focused, methodical plan, I got the entire problem solved by 3 p.m. It was a miracle how it unfolded.

I drove the car one mile to the paint and body shop at the end of Fontaine Drive. I explained that if I didn't get this scratch fixed by 3 p.m., I would be dead. I went on to say my stepfather was Carl Rivers, and they stopped me and said, "Say no more, we know of him." It didn't hurt that I was wearing a short skirt and a smile big enough to charm a snake. I begged them to help me, and they agreed. They asked if I would sign a waiver on the work, because it would not have enough time to dry. I told them I would sign in blood and give them a kiss upon delivery. Problem One solved; now on to the garage door, which was hanging by a hinge and had pulled away the wood framing attached to the house. I walked home, back down Fontaine Drive. "Think, think, think," as if I were Winnie the Pooh.

I didn't know much about the neighbor next door, except that he was in his mid-twenties and seemed to do nothing but lie around the house all day. We had waved at each other for the past ten years. I knocked on his door and pleaded, "Hey man, can you help me out? You know what an S.O.B. my stepfather is, and I've wrecked the car and torn up the garage door. Can you help me fix it before he gets home from work? The clock is ticking, and I only have four hours." Surprisingly, he looked up for the challenge. He got his Dad's toolbox and followed me next door to the wreckage. In no time, he had bent the arm back in place and repaired the frame with a new piece of 2' x 4' wood to replace the cracked mess. As he was hammering the last nail, I was painting. It was almost

2 p.m., and I asked him to drive me to the end of the road to pick up the repaired car. He laughed and told me I was an "amazing woman." I think that is the first time I was ever called a "woman." I told him I only wanted to see tomorrow; I wouldn't give Carl the pleasure of killing me. For years, he had witnessed Carl's angry fits.

The car looked great. You couldn't even tell where it was damaged, and the paint job looked awesome. Off I drove to pick up the girls and Mom from school. She was absolutely shocked that the car was fixed, and we vowed to keep this a secret (another one to manage). We agreed that we could survive the afternoon better if Carl wasn't screaming at us. But I feared that one day the fender paint would wipe off, so I made sure that I was the one who washed the car each week. The plan had succeeded; Carl never knew! As I washed the car, my neighbor next door gave me the thumbs up. And every time the garage door went up or down, I cringed. If it fell, I would pay dearly. It never did! Yet another miracle.

The Sweater

I spent that Christmas deeply depressed. I spiraled to a place where I could no longer even force a smile. I was so lonely; Jay never called, and I couldn't find a date to get me out of the house, away from the doom and gloom. I would have gone out with Quasimodo. I was not allowed to talk on the phone for more than sixty seconds! I was not allowed to have any friends over; I was not allowed to go to anybody's house and just hang out; and I was not allowed to go to the movies. I was in prison with no parole possible. To make matters worse, my Mother was lost in her annual Christmas depression.

I would sit and remember the few moments of fun I enjoyed with Jay. My dates were timed, and I had to go straight to my destination. I always feared we were being followed. Jay would go to elaborate means to make sure that didn't happen, and on my favorite dates, he took me to the lounge in the Ramada Inn where we would dance the night away. I sat alone in the strictly formal living room, remembering the soft music and Jay's arms around me, wearing the sympathy sweater my Mother had purchased months ago. The sweater was supposed to make me forget about the sixteen stitches in my head. She did the only thing she knew how to: she tried to purchase forgiveness -- a tactic she learned from Carl. When he hurt her, he bought her fancy gifts to make her forget, and she thought the sweater would make me forget. It didn't.

It was a hectic morning, as we dressed for the day. I begged my Mother to take me to the library to research a big term paper or let me drive there. I needed straight A's, as I was banking on a college scholarship for my ticket out of my hell on earth. She kept telling me, "You know Carl won't let you go to a library, and he won't let me take you, you'll just have to get it some other way." (This was long before the Internet was an available method of communication.)

I replied in a rebellious tone, "Are you a robot? Can you not stand up to him for once in your life?" As I was yelling this at a high pitch, I turned to walk away, only to feel a sharp pain in the back of my head. Within seconds, I felt the warm blood seep around my neck and flow down my chest. I'll never forget as long as I live, looking to my right into the large vanity mirror over the bathroom sink and seeing my Mother with the hand-held mirror raised above her head. She had gashed my head open with a silver-plated hand mirror. I saw stars like you see over Tweety Bird's head, and I felt faint at the sight of so much blood.

She started screaming at me, "Get in the tub so you don't get blood on my carpet!" My back slithered down the wall, and my knees wobbled as I sank into the tub, bleeding profusely. She gave me a towel and said she needed to get to work, as she was already late. "Carl will be home in a few minutes to get you a Band-aid." My crisp, white-oxford, Mobile Christian uniform shirt was soaked with blood, which had now started to roll down my forehead. I lay in the tub trying to assure my sisters I was okay, and that I'd get them breakfast in a few minutes. My head hurt so bad that I was scared, and my heart hurt so badly, my soul ached. The blood kept pouring, and I felt faint and nauseated at the same time. I really thought I might die. They would find me dead right there in the bathtub.

When Carl arrived home, he was stunned and started screaming profanities about my Mother; that she was a "sorry, gutless bitch" and a "g-d sorry excuse for a mother." He put some ice on my head, tried to stop the bleeding and gave me a towel to apply pressure. He told my sisters not to tell anyone at school what happened. I told him I needed to go to sleep, and he kept yelling at me to "keep your f-----g eyes open, or I'll have to take you to the emergency room!" He tried everything to stop the bleeding, but I was losing a lot of blood, and I passed out several times. I started to vomit, and I think it scared him. I think he really thought I was going to die, so he did muster up enough mercy to drive me to the hospital. The entire way there, he was yelling at me, "You don't f-----g need to cause us any more problems. You fell in the bathtub. Do you understand me, you fell in the bathtub?"

I arrived at the emergency room and recited that sentence fifty-five times. Carl would not leave my side. A couple of hours later, a nurse sneaked in after he had gone to the restroom and said, "We found glass in your head. What really happened? You can trust me. Just tell me and I'll help you."

My glazed eyes staring straight ahead, I gave my robotic reply, "I fell in the bathtub." Sixteen stitches later, we drove home in silence. A cat scan showed that I had a concussion, and my head throbbed from the pain. But my heart throbbed from the lies I told in the emergency room, all to protect the secret. I wished my Mother had succeeded. I wished I were going to my funeral instead of going home. All I wanted was to be seen, to be heard, and to be believed.

That afternoon I couldn't rest and recover; t she had to drag me to the store to buy me a sweater. That sweater stayed in my closet for years and years until one day, I threw it away. Whenever I wore it, I thought of its meaning. It was from the Levi store, and it had red stripes. How ironic.

CHAPTER 10

Terminal Moment

It was a Sunday, January 16, 1983, the beginning of the end--a day that changed my life forever, a day I will never forget as long as I live. I had no idea where he found the envelope, or where I found the valor. He pulled it from behind his back and began to wave it in my face screaming at the top of his lungs, "What the hell is this *g-d* envelope about? You little sorry bitch! You think they give a s--t about you?" His screams splattered me with his spit. I knew exactly the contents of the blue envelope he waved in my face.

My Grandmother Wells had sent me a Christmas card thanking me for my letter and the pictures I sent to her after our visit. I had included a wallet-sized school picture from every year so they could see what I looked like growing up. Somehow, I thought that would make them a part of my childhood. My Mother was yelling along with Carl, and I snapped. I had no words to defend myself, I could not take that he was screaming. I didn't know how to respond or what to do.

But I knew a few things: I knew my biological father left me. I knew he wouldn't even hold me after I was born. His attempts to see me were futile, and he surely didn't try hard enough. He didn't care enough. Had he made any significant effort, my fate could have been different. I'll never understand how he could walk away from his baby girl and never look back. He gave me up for adoption. He and his family turned their backs on me. This reality is emblazoned on my heart forever. The enjoyment Carl was taking in bashing this situation into my soul was the last straw. He didn't have that right. His sins against me were greater than theirs. He had no right, and I snapped. I didn't care if he killed me the next second. It didn't matter. Nothing mattered anymore. I didn't matter anymore. I didn't matter to anyone.

At that moment, his tirade and flailing did not scare me. I had no urge to run, no urge to hide. Instead, I was fed up, and a rage boiled over in me that made me blow.

"Hit me! Hit me, hard!" I screamed in his face. "Just f-----g kill me, you sick bastard! Just f-----g get it over with! Go ahead, kill me, please!" I ran out of the house, and he didn't follow. I was outside and still alive. I made it to the swing in the backyard, and I began to sway back and forth and kept repeating, "It's over. It's all over."

My Mother fried chicken, made rice and gravy and our standard can of LeSeur garden peas. She yelled for me to come to the table. I didn't even look up. I kept swinging and chanting, "It's over." I couldn't get my breath, I couldn't look up, and I couldn't go on. My head hung low as I swayed frozen inside.

Hours rolled by, and at about 2:30 p.m. Carl headed out the door to work. "Get your little ass in here and clean this garage. I'll deal with you when I get home," he screamed from the driveway. I heard the car engine turn over, and off to work he went. As the engine revved, I heard the car screech out of the driveway and felt a relief I never felt before. I truly began to believe it was over. I began to think thoughts I had never dared to think. I thought to myself that I would never have to see him again. I would take my life tonight and would never have to face his fury again—never have to hear the words that humiliated and degraded me. My Mother kept begging me to come inside and eat something. It was cold but I couldn't feel the chill. I didn't move. I kept swinging and chanting, "It's all over." Sundown faded to twilight, and I still swayed in numbness.

It was nearly 9 p.m. when, like a robot, I got up and went inside. I was wearing a pair of old blue jeans and a tee shirt, and my bare feet felt the cold earth below. Inside the house, everything was still and dim. My Mother loved to sleep, so most nights she was snoring by 9 p.m. I gathered what I needed: the half-empty vodka bottle from under the kitchen sink, my Mother's check book from inside the kitchen drawer, my diary to record my last thoughts, and the keys to the 1972 Grand Prix with white vinyl top.

I had to keep moving, determined to execute my plan. While I still had the courage, I had to keep the plan in motion. I didn't dare wake my Mother. I could hear her snoring and blew her a kiss from the doorway. I hurried out the back door, put the car in gear, and rolled it down the driveway. At the end of the drive, I turned the ignition and drove as fast as I could down Fontaine Drive, looking at the little white-brick house in the rear-view mirror. It got smaller and smaller as I shifted my eyes straight into the darkest of nights. I got to the stop sign at Highway 217 and made a right. I drove slowly and deliberately now, not wanting to draw attention to my flight. I proceeded with my plan, the perfect plan that unfolded in my head while on the swing. I wished I had remembered my shoes. My feet were cold. The gas tank registered empty, and I needed to buy the sleeping pills.

I pulled into a Quick Mart for gas and the pills. I filled up the tank, not knowing how far I would go, and went inside to purchase the pills. I quickly found two boxes of Sominex and made my way to the counter. I filled out the check and just needed to fill in the amount. "Ma'am we can't take that check. I don't think you're the person whose name is on this check." She obviously knew my Mother and thought my purchase strange.

From behind me a man's voice said, "Make the check out to me and I'll pay for you." To this day, I don't know who the man was or even what he looked like. Who in his right mind would let an obviously distraught teenager, barefoot in January, purchase two bottles of Sominex? Possibly one of satan's demons.

I crawled back into the car, scared out of my wits, but deliberate. I set out for the quarter mile, a make-out spot, remotely located in the woods on the outskirts of town. It was Sunday, and they wouldn't find my body until Friday night, date night. Neither my Mother nor Carl had any clue where this place was, so I could leave this world feeling safe. I turned down the narrow dirt road, hearing the crackle of the rocks under the tires and all the scary sounds of the night. When I turned off the ignition, I heard the loudest sound: silence. I was determined to end my life and relieved I had found the courage to make it this far. I was broken. I was ready to end the abuse once and for all.

For years, I had fantasized about dying. My self-hatred had so saturated me that I now felt I didn't deserve to live. I dreamed day after day of my demise. My mind drifted to the future. I was sure I would be in heaven in a few short hours. I was saved, and God knew the pain I was in and the hopelessness of my situation. This was probably His plan, so I could go to be with Him for eternity. This was the deliverance I prayed for, and now I prayed for strength to execute it. "God, please hear my groaning, and make this as peaceful as possible. God, please let me die and be with You in heaven. Please don't send me to hell, and please understand I have no other choice. I know all about heaven from church and I want to float on a cloud. I want to live in the mansion You've prepared for me and I want to experience Your glory." I prayed for peace and not pain, I prayed for deliverance, and I prayed for those I would leave behind.

I took a sip of vodka from the bottle, and at first taste, it burned like fire, then turned to a warm, soothing feeling as it rolled down my throat and into my stomach. The taste of the liquor warmed my whole body. It eased my hunger pains, as I had not put a bite in my mouth all day. I tore open the box of sleeping pills and gnawed the plastic off of the bottle with my teeth, biting fiercely. Out came the cotton, and I placed the first pill on my tongue with a swig of vodka to wash it down. I pulled out my diary and remembered that I still had the pen that I had used to sign the check. I began to write what I thought would be my last thoughts, my last words, something that might be read at my funeral.

Journal Entry January 13, 1983

Another dream is dead. It's really over. Jay's got someone else, and I'm glad. Nobody needs to be messed up with me. I'm such an awful person. God, how I hate myself! I wish I were dead, then that'd solve all my problems. My parents hate me because I looked the Wells up. They wouldn't even give me a chance to explain. That man took joy in telling me how they left me when I was a baby. How they didn't care or love me or want me. He really rubbed it in. I hate him for ruining my life. He's destroyed every part of me and now he's destroyed my last dream. The dream that I had a daddy somewhere who loved me. I don't have one. I don't have anyone but me, and I hate me. If you ever read this, Mother, I want you to know that I love you more than life itself. You're the best mother a girl could have, so don't blame yourself! It's my fault – I could never talk to you. We were so close, yet we were so far away. You don't understand me, and you'll never be able to. I spent a lifetime trying to keep you from getting hurt, but I'm not strong enough to go on. I know you loved me, but I really never belonged. I was a problem from birth. You four will do just fine without me. Please never let my sisters forget how much I loved them. Please Mama, don't be sad and please don't cry 'cuz I'm in heaven now, and I don't have any more problems. I'm happy, and I want you to be happy, too. If you ever want to know the real reason why I did this, call Nicole.

Well, Angie, looks like you're really gonna' do it. Let's hope you have guts enough to do it right this time. I'm really messed up inside, and I'll never be able to be okay. I've held on for so long, but I think it's time now to let go. I've run out of dreams. They're all dead. They're all dead. They're all dead. Nobody cares. Nobody cares. Nobody cares, I'm gonna' do it tonight. I'm gonna' do it tonight. I'm gonna' do it tonight. I'm gonna' do it tonight. I'm gonna' do it tonight.

I imagined the police finding me dead in the car with my diary on my lap. If anyone would read between the lines, the diary held the story, and he would be punished, punished by the guilt of killing me, and I took joy in knowing that I would haunt him for the rest of his life. I filled my hand with the pills and took them as fast as I could swallow, washing each handful down with the vodka. The deadly combination relaxed me into slow motion. I turned on the radio, and "I Love to Love You, Baby" was playing. I dug in the seat beside me for the second box of pills, my hands patting the seat in the dark to find the second box that would seal my fate. I felt so light-headed, my arms became so heavy, and the dashboard began to wave. Everything became blurry. I knew I had to work fast and stay focused, because I had to get the second bottle down to make sure I would die. It was a struggle to get it open. In desperation, I got it open and ingested the pills in handfuls. As I did, I fought to find the lever to lay the white vinyl bucket seat back. I tried to breathe deeply, but the air was leaden as it entered my body, as if it were smog.

My arms were so heavy they felt as if they were coated with cement; my movement was slow and deliberate. I had to focus so hard on every move. I began to sink into the seat. The seat felt like marshmallows. I felt a celestial pull. I was falling very slowly, though. I was at peace and the seat was wrapping its arms around me. I closed my eyes and the light was bright, so bright it hurt, and I struggled to open my eyes. They were so heavy, so very heavy.

Was I dreaming, or was I dying? I didn't know. I knew no pain, only peace. I felt my breath slipping away. I focused on my breathing, and it was getting harder and harder to inhale. I focused --breathe in, breathe out. I was calm; I was at peace. I pulled in as deep a breath as I could, and then I felt my body rise up and I slouched against the door. The door fell open, and I hit the cold dirt. I don't remember reaching for the door handle. I didn't feel the cold chrome handle in my hand. To this day, I don't know how the door opened. I believe it to be a miracle. I hit the dirt hard, and the cold air of the January night hit me.

The cold air breathed life into me, shocked me, and I began to vomit violently. I couldn't move. I could feel cold air on my arms, but I couldn't feel my legs. I couldn't get up or move at all. I laid there paralyzed, vomiting and choking. I barely had the strength to turn my head to the side. My body pressed against the cold dirt. I began to shake violently. I had no control over any part of my body. I vomited and convulsed for what seemed like hours. I was conscious, but I couldn't move my body. I believed I was dying. This was not the peaceful death

I had prayed for, but if this was what I had to endure to die, then so be it. I thought I would go to sleep and wake up in heaven looking down on the mess I had left behind. I stopped puking and just lay there, waiting to die. I passed out thinking, "Okay, this is it." Saying goodbye to this world, I slept on the ice-cold January earth beneath me.

Desperation and Despair

"Oh my God!" I woke up some time later in the night. "Oh my God!" I panicked. I was covered in vomit that had the most pungent smell. I began to scream in agony. "God, please, no! No! I had to die! Please God, I had to die! I don't know what I'm going to do now! God I can't live!"

How could I not be dead? "Oh God, please, I had to die!" I wept. I beat the cold ground with my fists. My screams echoed back in my ear through the tall pine trees. I was at the end of my rope. In my distress, all I could think of was that I could never go back. All I could think of was Carl killing me, and I wouldn't give him that satisfaction. "I can never go back," I softly whispered. "Please God, please don't make me go back."

I crawled back into the car out of the freezing night air. I began to emerge from the haze, but I was still in despair. I had to kill myself before morning, and the clock was ticking. Feeling such a failure, I had to figure out a sure-fire end. How could someone take two bottles of sleeping pills, drink a half a bottle of vodka, and live? How could that be? Why can't I kill myself? I had the guts. I was sinking into the seat, I saw the light, but what happened? How did the car door open? All I remember is leaning forward. Why did I open my eyes when I saw the light? I would not give up. I can do this. I will die.

I was still a bit intoxicated, my vision blurred and my head pounding, but I managed to turn the keys in the ignition and drive to the Turner Bridge. I coached myself: "I can climb to the top of the bridge and jump into the Mobile River. I can't swim, so I won't survive."

It was the dead of the night, and the roads were deserted. Panicked, I sped to the crest of the bridge and turned off the car. The chilled pavement burned my bare feet, and the steel beams of the bridge were bitter ice. I began to climb the steel beams of the bridge. I climbed in frenzy and fear, as far up as my strength would carry me, and looked down into the black abyss. I got very dizzy. This would have been so much easier had I not been terrified of heights and even more terrified of deep water. The black waters of the river swirled beneath me, and terror filled my body. It was so cold, and I was so scared that my body shook and shuddered. I took hold of one of the bridge beams. I couldn't let go. I lacked the courage to let go of that frozen steel beam, and I also lacked the courage to let go of a life I couldn't hold onto. I slithered down the steel beams and sat on the freezing pavement. I couldn't cry anymore; I hadn't the strength. I could only pant. The night was slipping away from me, and I had nowhere to turn. I sat there in the cold night, broken to smithereens.

A semi-truck ripped by, blowing a strong wind, and I got an idea. I could get back into the car and drive over the Turner Bridge on the wrong side of the road. I could run head-on into one of these semis and would be killed instantly. I could floor the gas pedal when I got to the top of the bridge. If I didn't succeed at first, it wouldn't take me many times to hit. There were many trucks on the road going to the Port Authority, and the Turner Bridge connected Alabama to Florida. It would be gruesome, maybe even painful, but it was my last chance. I had no time to devise another plan. There was no time to tarry, as I had to be dead before the sun came up. I was so very tired. My body felt like it had already been run over by a semi-truck. Feeling like a total failure, I crawled back into the car, ready to succeed, ready to get this night over with, a night that was turning out to be the worst night of my life.

I started over the bridge in slow gear and then began accelerating as I crossed over to the opposite lane. I was looking for a head-on collision. It would be a quick end of me. Suddenly, a gruesome thought flashed through my mind: "Oh God, I may kill someone else. I can't kill an innocent person for my own satisfaction." As I reached the top of the bridge, I jerked the steering wheel back into my lane. I was heading into Florida and now had officially crossed the state line. I could keep driving, but horror overwhelmed me. I had only a checkbook that, I assure you, had a single-digit balance, and less than a half -tank of gas. I was wearing a tee shirt and blue jeans and barefoot in the dead of winter. I reeked of vomit from my hair to my toes. It would be difficult to get a job looking like this. Maybe I could find a convenience store open and buy a razor blade. Then I could slit my wrists.

I pulled over and sat there in the dark. I didn't know what time it was, so I turned on the radio. The disc jockey finally announced it was half past 4 a.m. I had left home around 9:30 p.m., and I felt as though I had lived through a week. "My God in heaven, what do I do? I am at the end of my rope and you won't let me let go. I am so scared and too terrified to run, yet too terrified to turn back. How do I go on? How do I make it through this day? I am desperate--so desperate-- and I am sad, and I don't know where to turn or what to do."

I could barely breathe in and out. I wanted to stop breathing. My chest was so heavy, and my head pounded. I thought about driving to a hospital. I thought about just driving -- driving off the face of the earth. I still had the checkbook, but I knew there wasn't much money in the account. I remember a feeling coming over me that was beyond me, beyond anything I can explain in human terms. It was as if a warm blanket was wrapped around my shoulders, and I heard the words in my head, "We'll figure it out" Who was 'we'? "Is that you, God?"

I had to go to the bathroom so badly, that I squatted outside the car in the dark, petrified. Suddenly, the address of my friend, Nicole, came to me. How I remembered her exact address is a miracle. Nicole was the only friend I ever confided in about my sexual abuse. She had also been sexually abused by a family friend. She shared my pain, and I swore her to secrecy, as she did me.

I zipped up my pants and jumped in the car with a glimmer of hope that I could find her house. I knew the general vicinity, but had never been there. I didn't know what else to do, but I thought that maybe her parents would let me stay with them until I could figure it out. Maybe they wouldn't ask too many questions. I didn't have any options, so I headed back over the bridge in search of her house. Luckily, Mobile streets are laid in a grid, and I found the house with ease. It was almost 5 a.m. and dark as I pulled into the drive. I waited in the drive for the lights in the house to come on. I was able to close my eyes for a few minutes and ease the throbbing in my head. I glanced at the awful mess in the car. There was vomit all over the seat from my clothes and the empty packages of the sleeping pills. I took a deep breath and saw the lights of the house turn on. Here I go. I hurried out of the car before I lost my nerve. A huge, burly man I had never seen before answered the door with a look of anger.

I said, "My name is Angie, and I need to see Nicole."

He said, "Nicole is still sleeping, but come on in and talk to me."

"Please," I begged, "I just need to talk to Nicole," as I began to weep uncontrollably.

"I'll wake her", and he disappeared into the back of the house. He came back and led me to Nicole's bedroom. I asked if he would please let us talk privately. He reluctantly agreed and left us alone. I could barely speak for crying.

She understood about every third word, but quickly saw my despair and said, "It's okay. My Dad will figure it out." A calm wrapped around me as I heard those words again in my head. Nicole left and came back with her mother and father, who unbeknownst to me, was one of the most powerful attorney's in Mobile.

"Tell him everything, Angie."

I began to spill my guts, and by the end of my story, he had compartmentalized all my issues and had a plan of action.

"First, I'll call your parents. They're certain to have contacted the police. Next, I'll transport you to my Mother's house where you can't be traced. Third, I'll petition the judge for your independent guardianship. Fourth, we'll confront your stepfather, and he'll be punished for what he has done to you."

Nicole's mother was a soft-spoken woman and offered to help me clean up. Things become extremely blurry during the next few hours. I think my mind shut down, as I now had help. I remember only bits and pieces, but I am sure Nicole's Dad can fill in the blanks for me one day.

I gave him my home phone number to call, and he left the room to call to my home and his mother. I don't remember driving to her house, but it was a condo, and I was given some clothes and took a long, hot shower. She gave me the most comfortable bed with a down comforter. I sank into it and gave up. I wasn't in control anymore. I had survived the worst night of my life, and now I needed some sleep to get through the worst day of my life that was ahead.

Early afternoon, I was awakened with a tray of food. Above me stood Nicole's grandmother, an attractive elderly lady, with soft, long gray waves of hair surrounding her face, and sporting a gentle smile. She touched my face tenderly and said, "It's all going to be okay. We're going to figure it all out." No one had ever touched my cheek that way. I could feel the love travel through her fingertips. I had no choice but to trust. She explained to me that the police had picked up the car I stole, and returned it to my family. I started to cry. The tender old grandmother said, "Please don't cry. It's going to be fine, I promise."

I explained to her that the car was left in a mess from last night and that my diary was still in the car. I needed my diary.

"My Mother can't read my diary."

She broke the news, "Your Mother has been told."

The SECRET! I could barely breathe and certainly couldn't keep eating. I pushed the tray away, as I hyperventilated. She ran and got me a paper bag and instructed me to breathe slowly. She begged me to eat, but I couldn't. She said that Nicole's Mom was coming for me soon and that my parents were going to meet me at Nicole's dad's law office. I didn't want to see them; I didn't want to go. I wanted to stay here for the rest of my life. I had no choice in the matter.

She got Nicole's dad on the phone, and he explained to me very slowly that my parents had hired a prominent attorney in Mobile. He explained that I needed to trust him, and I had to make a decision on prosecuting Carl. Prosecuting Carl? That had never crossed my mind. Last night I wanted to die. Now with the sun shining through the window, I so wanted my freedom. I wanted him to leave me alone. I wanted him to leave my Mother alone. He proceeded to tell me that I would need to take a lie detector test immediately, because my Mother was denying that this could have possibly happened. He told me that Carl had denied everything and had declined to take the test. Nicole's dad told me not to be afraid, and that I didn't have to see Carl. He said he would put me in a room and let my Mother come in and talk to me, and then I could decide how I wanted him to represent me. I didn't want to go. I wanted another bottle of sleeping pills ...

CHAPTER 11

Faith to Float

On the river, with the protection of the raft, a life jacket and a helmet, I'm ready to conquer the treacherous waters, to visit my old friend fear, to take life to the edge. The adventure starts out as a cakewalk. The first leg is smooth sailing, rolling through gentle rapids; a few passable falls, paddle right, paddle left, then we roll over another whitecap rapid, and then dive into the spinning water. Then the guides start screaming, "This one is Corkscrew, paddle hard, all together now, keep paddling, hard I say!" The dive is deeper, the drop is rough, and water pours over the sides of the raft, soaking each of us. I look back with great pride and hold my paddle high over my head in victory.

We finally face the most challenging rapid: Bull Sluice. "This is a Class five, so give it all you've got! This one will show me what you're made of today, so paddle hard and listen close to my directions. Go! Go! Go! Hard right, hard right!" I have lost my stomach at the long drop, and then I am under water. Violent rapids knock me out of the raft. Water pours over my head and rushes up my nose, burning. I can't see, and I can't breathe. I fight to get to the surface. I fight to catch a breath …the tremendous undertow pulls my legs and I am fighting, clawing, and whaling my arms to get to the surface. The struggle is tremendous, and I am under again, not knowing if I will ever come up. The tow of the hydraulic takes me deeper into another dimension of struggle. I fight even harder. My legs are sucked down under the rocks. I breathe in water, and I begin to choke. I remember the crash course: lift up your feet, hold your vest, keep your head up and just float, and "we'll get to you."

"Don't fight the river, don't swim, just float." That is easier said than done when you're being sucked down. The harder you try to get your feet up, the more you struggle, as your entire body is being beaten by the rocks and the racing waters.

Fellow rafters are screaming at me, but I can't hear their words. The rope is thrown to me, but I can't get to it. I remember this feeling that I can only describe as the *"undertow of life"* that had sucked me down before. I am near death, yet holding on to life, a life that God had ordained and saved for His glory, and a life that He has given me the power to fight for and heal from. The struggle never ends.

The river pulled me under, but my faith pulled me up, like the safety instructions on the lifejacket said. The river guides taught me to pull my legs up and float, not fight, struggle or try to swim. *"Flip over on your back and get your legs up out of the water, toes up."* That's how you survive the river. It's not in your power, but in your faith. I hear their screams, *"Flip over on your back and float and look for the rope!"* I had faith to turn over. Still choking from the water, I catch my breath. I emerge victorious over the river and my fears.

The rafting journey and the near drowning reminded me of that fateful Mobile night when I had faced death. I don't know what I would have done without Nicole's family's help. I have thought about that suicide attempt so many times. After failing miserably, I began to think that maybe God had a specific assignment for my life. Nicole's dad listened to my cry for help. I realized suicide was a way to flee my memories, my pain, and mostly myself. It was the easy way out. It was the coward's way out. It was a cry for help, and thank God, Nicole's dad heard it. I have learned that true bravery comes in facing the truth and having a faith and trust in God that He is with you, even in the darkest, coldest fear under the water of the river or the weight of the world. Life is in His hands and His hands alone.

Rejection and Rejuvenation

I can barely write what took place over the next few hours. I had arrived at Nicole's father's law office physically exhausted after the night I'd endured. I could not stop shaking. My body quivered from fear and exhaustion. The stress of the night, the sleeping pills, and the alcohol's effects were still in my system. I was sitting upright in a chair when my Mother entered the room. She showed no mercy but immediately lit into me. She screamed that I had set in motion a chain of events that would now ruin her life. She blasted me with both barrels:

"You have ruined my life. How could you do this? How could you embarrass and destroy our family? You must be on drugs. You're shaking like you're on drugs. I knew you were on drugs. You've become a drug addict." She never let me open my mouth. She continued to berate me, her eyelids blinking frantically, as I sat in the chair with my head hung down low. "I've contacted the Wells, and they said they would take you. You can go there this afternoon and leave us alone. This can't be true. It's all a lie. You are a liar. You're a big liar." She was fireball-red from the top of her chin all the way down her neck with red blotches screaming anger and fear out of her skin.

She would have hit me had she not thought she was being monitored closely. I could tell she wanted to rip me to pieces. She could have pulled every hair out of my head, and that still wouldn't have solved her problems. She told me I could come to the house and gather my things, but I needed to make it fast. "You don't need to put us through anymore today. We've had a horrible night. You have really ruined our lives, and I want you as far away from me as possible, out of our lives for good. I want you out. I don't even know who you are. You are not the little girl I raised and loved. You are not the little girl I sacrificed my life for. I've called the Wells, and they're going to take you in. You can go there as soon as you get your stuff, and I don't want to see you ever again. You need to be with the Wells. You need to be with them now! Maybe they can figure you out," her voice quivered.

Her eyelids were batting faster, as they always did when she was nervous, her voice was stern and detached, and her neck was covered with red blotches. There was no sympathy in her tone. There was no wavering in her decision. I had told the unthinkable, the unbelievable, and her response was to bury herself in denial. The reality of what was happening at that moment was more than I could process. She turned her back to me, and even more heartbreaking, turned her back *on* me.

She walked out and slammed the door. Nicole's father must have known I needed a few minutes, so I was left alone in the cold conference room. I was flabbergasted. I did not even have the strength to lift my head up. Never did I ever imagine she would turn her back on me. That was the final blow. The worst blow I could have received. "Why God? Why didn't you take me last night? Why is there no end to my suffering?" My soul had been ripped out, my heart shattered to a million pieces. My Mother didn't love me enough to fight for me, to believe me. I'd spent years enduring the unbearable, all those years protecting her and protecting the secret. She chose him. She turned her back on me and chose him. She betrayed me. I had no one and nowhere to go. I wasn't going to Danbury. The Wells' left me and never looked back. They walked out of my life. I wasn't going to beg them to take me in. I didn't need them. I didn't need anybody.

The door opened and Nicole's father towered over me, as my head was still hanging between my legs. "You have to make a decision. We can seek justice. I need to know what to do, and I need to know right now." His stern, deep voice shocked me back into reality.

"Can I have some time to think this through? I've protected them for so long. I never wanted her to know. I never wanted to hurt her like this."

He stayed on his point as a lawyer: "I'm sorry, but you have to make a move now. I have no choice because you are a minor. You have to focus on *you* now. I will prosecute. We can put him behind bars, we can get justice," he urged in a deep firm tone.

"There is no justice in this, no justice," I said. "I just want my freedom. Please get me my freedom. I don't want anything but my freedom, please," I whispered in a soft crackling voice. "Just my freedom. Please get me my freedom, and I'll go as far away from this place as I can get. I promise, please just let me out of this hell, please let it be over."

He saw the utter despair in my face, and the total hopelessness of my situation. Out of pity, he asked if I wanted to stay with them a few days until we figured things out. I was in such a pitiful state; he had no choice but to extend a hand. I thought I was at the end of my rope on the bridge last night, and within a few hours, I had slipped even further down. There was no fight left in me. I was tired, I was alone, and I was defeated. I truly know what it feels like to be at the end of yourself and sitting on the bottom of life. At that moment, I had no more of *me* to depend on; I had only God. All I had was blind faith and a verse I clung to: "I can do all things through Christ who strengthens me." (Philippians 4:13)

Within what seemed like minutes, I was getting my emancipation in front of a judge and my petition for freedom granted. "Get your education and make sure to make something of yourself," said the judge. "Don't let this ruin your life. You can rise above. Many others have done so," he continued. Nicole's father assured him he would seek therapy for me, and I would be living with them for a while.

Nicole drove me to 465 Briar Patch Place. Mom, Carl and my two sisters peered through the window as we got out of the car. The reception was cold. It took less than ten minutes to gather my belongings. I was given two black trash bags. My heart raced with fear and exhaustion. Carl stayed out of my way, my

Mother cried, and my sisters clung to my legs, pleading for me not to leave them.

I was so angry, so fiercely angry, as I shoved my clothes into the bag and grabbed my eight-track player and all my eight tracks. I asked if I could take my bicycle, and they agreed. I found my schoolbooks, but not my diary.

"Can I have my diary please?" She said she didn't know where it was. "It was in the car last night," I replied.

"No, you can't have your diary. It's gone. He burned it in the ditch this morning." [The diary, it turns out, was not destroyed, and miraculously, years later, I was able to find it, well hidden under the armoire in the master bedroom at 465 Briar Patch Place. The "Journal" entries within this book came from this diary.]

Her reply didn't register, as I needed to get out of there immediately before I started doing dishes or making the beds or worse, grabbing a butcher knife and going stark raving mad. I had to get out of there before I buckled, before I wrapped my arms around my sisters, thinking that I needed to stay to protect them more than I needed to go to protect myself. Leaving them behind made my gut ache. I wrapped my arms around them, held them close and said, "You both look me in the eye now. I love you, and I'll be back to see you. You can call me at this number if you need me, and I'll be back to see you. Be good. I'll be back, I swear, I'm not leaving for good. Just a little while, and I'll be back." Tears streamed down their cheeks. "Please don't cry, please," I pleaded.

I had to leave my bicycle behind, as I threw the bags in the back of Nicole's Toyota Supra. She said, "Help me take the tee-tops off. I have an idea." We took the tee-tops off, and she told me to stand up in the front seat and scream to the top of my lungs. She said, "Experience your freedom. Scream 'I'm free!'"

There was a mass in my throat. I couldn't talk. I choked, but in a matter of seconds, I went manic as I screamed and screamed – all the way down Fontaine Drive and all the way down Highway 217. She drove me all over town for hours screaming. It felt so good. I was free, and I had so much to scream about. I laughed, I cried, and I screamed. She was the best friend a girl could have. She kept driving, and I kept screaming all the way down Victory Drive (that was its name and it symbolized what I was experiencing!)

This was so very different for me. Often I would let my breakdowns explode inside my head, and I would scream silently. But now, thanks to Nicole, the screams were boiling out. And now, also thanks to Nicole, I felt release. She smiled at me as she drove, and I enjoyed the freedom to scream. I enjoyed the freedom to smile.

CHAPTER 12

Flight to Freedom

So I stayed with Nicole. We were opposites, and I guess there is some truth that opposites attract. We grew close while we were on the yearbook staff together. She towered almost six feet tall and was a big girl, not fat, but athletic. She was a talented basketball player. She had beautiful green eyes and blonde hair that hung straight on her shoulders with a weather wave. The humidity would make it frizzy. She was very opinionated and very confident and shared an enormous sense of humor. She was my best friend. She could make me laugh through anything, a bellyache laugh that often got us in trouble in high school when we couldn't control our giggles. She didn't exactly treat me like her best friend, but I knew she was mine.

I clung to Nicole every chance I got in school. I would sit with her at lunch, and we would hang out afterward in the courtyard. We talked about serious things, and we shared a sadness layered beneath the surface because Nicole confided in me that she was also sexually abused. We shared a bond in that pain that could never be broken. Now in a strange twist of events her father - in a single day - had become my hero.

I felt as though I had been transported to another planet. Nicole's home was stately, yet warm and cozy; it was spacious and inviting. We could wear our shoes in the house, unlike my home. We could sit on the couch and even lounge on it. They laughed,

142

teased, and hugged. They exercised and read; they sat around and talked over a meal about current events and about school. They truly cared about one another's feelings. It all felt so foreign to me.

I showed up at school on Tuesday morning with Nicole. Everyone had questions, and I answered, "I'm staying with Nicole for a while." I already had enough credits to graduate, so Nicole's dad gave me a job in the afternoon at his law office. I worked diligently to earn my keep. He started me in therapy immediately. I hated therapy. My therapist would give me ink blots to describe. I didn't see how that would help me get over a childhood of sexual abuse, of what was a lifetime of being ravaged daily. She looked all of thirty and seemed as though her biggest trauma was a hangnail. While I believe therapy to be worthwhile, I could not come to grips with the value of identifying ink blots or how this therapist would return my dignity and self-worth, all of which had been robbed. No one could replace my innocence, no one could erase the years of words and actions that ripped me apart from the inside out. No one could wipe clean my childhood slate of abuse.

Now I was abandoned by my Mother. No one could get inside my head, no one could truly understand what I was feeling, and no one, as hard as they tried, could replace the love I'd lost. No ink blot description could do that. I missed my Mother terribly, and a part of me missed the madness. There was a void; there was a suffering that ached inside me. I couldn't stop thinking that somehow all this was my fault. Maybe if I had only been born ugly, or better yet, not been born at all, then none of this would have happened.

I began to stroll down a road of self-destruction. I didn't care anymore. I ached for the emptiness in my heart to go away. I wanted someone to nurture me, and if only for an hour, to somehow ease my pain. I continued to manipulate to get what I wanted and never considered the consequences, partly because of my immaturity and partly because I was experiencing a freedom I had never known, a freedom that had no boundaries. When you have suffered through sexual abuse, you end up with shifting boundaries, and true ethics are scrambled. In stark contrast to my home life, Nicole's family was bonded in trust. They never considered that they could not trust me, and as a result, I put myself in places where I had no business being, with people I had no business being with, all for a few moments of attention and thrill.

Nicole's sister, Jenny, came home from college for a weekend visit and was disturbed to find me sleeping in her bedroom. She put up quite a fuss, and I was quickly relocated to a storage room off of the garage that had been turned into a library. There was a daybed and built-in floor to ceiling bookshelves surrounding the room, but it was lonely and cold. I was detached from the family nucleus. This bland room was a roof over my head, but not a place to recover from the destruction of my childhood. When I was living in Jenny's room, I was in the center of the hall between Nicole's room and her parents. They were always checking on me, just coming in to see how I was doing. I felt like an outsider looking in, and I began a new diary.

Journal Entry March 27, 1983

I've been so depressed this weekend because I really miss my Mom. I don't fit in anywhere. I rescheduled my piano lesson Saturday so mine would run into hers thinking she'd talk to me for a while or invite me to get ice cream with them like we used to, but she didn't. After I saw my Mom on Saturday, I was so very sad and started thinking about the night I tried to kill myself. Sometimes, I wish I had succeeded, but other times I really enjoy life. Sometimes, I don't understand why I feel the way I feel. I am so mixed up.

I knew my time was coming to an end at Nicole's house, and to facilitate things, Nicole and I got into a teenage tiff that sent me packing on a sour note. Tension had been building for weeks, as her parents caught me in one tale after another. I disrupted the dynamics in their family. My issues were more than anyone could handle. Their home was not the place to purge my hurt. Like every family, they struggled with life's issues.

My problems only created more turmoil and stress for their family. They didn't deserve to be forced to take ownership of this troubled teen and all her baggage. I moved out a couple of weeks before graduation and moved in with my Aunt Hazel and Uncle Chip a few miles away on the outskirts of Mobile.

Uncle Chip was the sweetest man you'd ever meet, and he treated me like one of his own. The house was crowded, to say the least, with their children coming and going; but my aunt, knowing I had nowhere else to turn, opened her doors and made me feel at home.

I knew if I could only get my diploma, I would be off to college, out of everyone's hair and out of Mobile for good, with no desire to ever return except for perhaps a brief visit, but never to live. I wanted to run as far as I could from my past and to just forget I dreamed of making a life for myself, a clean sweep, void of my past. I dreamed of standing on my own two feet able to take care of myself.

Journal Entry April 14, 1983

One day rolls into the next, and life seems to be passing by. Sometimes, I think I'll never be normal. Spring break ended today and life's going back to routine. I really enjoyed the time I spent with my grandma. We had fun fishing and quilting, my Granny's two great loves. I love her so much because she makes me feel special. I love Mom too, but I think she has stopped loving me. I feel so betrayed. After all, I went through – all I put up with for all those years, and she turns her back on me now. Now, when I needed her more than ever, she was invisible. She looks through me. She doesn't believe me. How can she even call herself my Mother? All those years I took on her responsibilities, I worked so hard to earn her love. This is the thanks I get. I get so scared sometimes. So afraid of the future – of being alone, but then I think I can't get much more alone than I am right now. I may not be alone, but I feel very lonely. It's me against the world, and if I fail, they'll all get a big laugh. I can't fail. I can never let anyone know

146

that my fear of failing exists. I'm so full of fear that I can't seem to ever get rid of it... Fear of being alone, fear of failing and fear of letting him destroy me. I'll destroy him first. I don't know how, where, or when, but one day I'm going to gain sweet vengeance. I'd kill him right now if I knew I wouldn't go to prison for it. I'd love to shoot him right between the eyes ten times and have him begging me to stop each time. I hate him. I hate his guts for ruining my life. I want to make his life as totally miserable as he's made mine. Rather than killing him, I'd like to see him suffer. As for my Mother – I'll never forgive her for this. I can't see how she can go to bed with a man who abused her own daughter. But sometimes I don't feel like her daughter. Sometimes, I feel like a real nobody.

I needed so desperately to stay in touch with my real family. I needed to make sure Mother and my young sisters were okay. I had spent my days protecting them, and I couldn't turn my back on them now. I was out and I was safe. They were not. I feared for each of them. My sisters were his biological children, and I prayed that was enough to keep him at bay. I wanted him to know he had to leave them alone, or I would bust his chops wide open.

For the first months after I left home, he let my Mother quit work, and he bought her every fine item under the sun: anything she wanted, anything that would purchase her compliance. He took her on elaborate shopping trips and convinced her that I was a liar. She was so weak that, merely to have the peace, to experience his silenced devil-tongue and to enjoy her nice new things, was worth sending me away. They all seemed happier than ever that I was gone.

I was so angry. I was the bad guy, the deceiver. In her sick mind, she believed I made all this up. I was to blame. I was always to blame. A child of three, four, five, six, seven, eight, and nine years of age was to blame for all the abuse I suffered. "Yes," she clucked, "it's your fault." They were making me out to be a vicious liar. I hated every second I spent with them, so I convinced them to let me take my sisters on short excursions away from 465 Briar Patch Place. I took them to the movies, I took them to the circus, I entertained them, and they loved spending time with me. I could barely stomach time with my Mother, as much as I wanted to be with her. I felt the need to justify myself and my actions. She was blind and buried behind a thick veil of self-righteousness. She was in a dungeon of denial, and nothing I said mattered. She didn't care. Her world was secure, so I didn't matter. She said many times, "You will survive."

Survival was an art I had mastered. I wondered if it was my fault for not opening my mouth the first time it happened. But if I had spoken, what would I have said? Now I know that it was in no way my fault, but it was the responsibility of the adults in my life. I can't turn back time. I can't unravel the maze of manipulations that brought me to this place. I can't go back. I can only put one foot in front of another and look for a sweet red sucker and a milkshake to sooth me. Terrified to return home, and terrified for my sisters if I abandoned them, I would force myself to muster the courage to visit on occasion. I put them first, and I returned. Always trying to schedule my visit around Carl's absence, I sometimes failed and was forced to face him. In his presence, I returned to the damaged little girl.

> *Journal Entry April 17, 1983*
> *I spent the afternoon at home [465 Briar Patch Place]. It felt so good to be in my own home with familiar surroundings. I can't seem to stop crying. A part of me wanted to stay. It's the only place that I really feel as though I fit. Carl was super nice; sugar wouldn't melt in his mouth. I ate supper with them and felt really at home. It's like nothing's happened and an eerie calmness hung in the air. We talked about general things and even laughed. Sometimes, I think I'm happier playing a game than living reality. I feel so lonely and empty inside. I wish I had someone who really cared about me. Anybody. I wish I had Jay back.*

Finding Tomorrow

It was graduation night, the end of a season, and I had been chosen to give the commencement address for my class. I worked long hours on the speech and was ready to deliver it. I was living what I was about to share. For the moment, I could see freedom and a new life ahead.

"... My fellow classmates and honored guests, I'd like to welcome you to commencement exercises for the class of 1983. We've approached this day with a tremendous amount of anticipation. Today marks the end of twelve years of a continuous cycle of learning, growing, and changing. With one hand, we are closing the door to yesterday. We leave behind all the wonderful memories of school. But with the other hand, we are opening the door to the long and winding road to our future. We will each venture down different paths, but graduation is only a milestone in our learning process. Learning is a life-long privilege. It is not a journey. It is not a destination. It is not a task to be completed, but a process to be continued. We cannot train ourselves once and feel educated. What was right and plausible yesterday is questionable today and might even be wrong tomorrow. In our society, knowledge is accumulating so fast that we must run to stand still.

"The class of 1983 stands before you with the potential to be anything they desire. As Longfellow put it, 'the future is only limited by us.' Whatever your mind can conceive and believe, you will achieve. There exist limitless opportunities in every industry.

"Where there is an open and willing mind, there will always be a frontier. You must not only act but also dream; not only plan, but also believe. Defeat may test you, but it need not stop you. There is no failure except in no longer trying. If at first you don't succeed, try another way. Epicurus once said, 'The greater the difficulty, the more glory in surmounting it. For every obstacle you may face, somewhere, somehow there is a solution.' The greatest mistake in the world is giving up. Success is never final and failure never fatal. It's the courage to keep on trying that counts.

"Wishing will not bring success, but planning, persistence and a burning desire deep within will. Success is a journey, not a destination. The journey of a thousand miles begins with a single step. I challenge each member of the class of 1983 to take that first step today."

My knees knocked, and my voice cracked as I looked out over the dimly lit crowd. I saw Nicole's dad peering at me with a blank stare: the man who won my emancipation, the man whom I owe a tremendous debt of gratitude for opening his door. I saw my Mother, whose sad eyes locked on my every word. I saw an old lady waving her four fingers at me: a stranger who acts like she knows me. I continued trying to communicate the best I could, trying to believe the words that were departing my lips, that I would survive and that I would embrace my future with excitement and hope, trying to inspire my peers standing behind me. If I could convince myself then, I could surely convince the blank faces that stared back at me from the crowd.

As soon as my speech was delivered, it received a standing ovation. I was overwhelmed and suddenly felt a confidence I had never known. Were they cheering for me, my speech, or my peers? It didn't matter because I could now reach for tomorrow. I flung my graduation cap straight up in the air, and as I caught it, I can remember thinking to myself, "You are going to make it – you are! 'You are going to make it with wings,' as my Granny always chanted. This is the first day of the rest of your life."

I was walking out of the auditorium to greet my family, when out of the crowed a silver-haired lady came barreling toward me calling out "Precious! Precious Angela!" She flailed her arms and flung them around my neck, squeezing so tight I couldn't breathe.

She said she had waited a lifetime to meet me. She hugged me and continued to squeeze as she kissed my face a hundred times. She panted in a giggly voice with such excitement, "Precious, you are mine now." All this affection made me uncomfortable. I didn't know what to say, but I wanted to ask, 'Who are you and where did you come from, and are you sure you have the right Angela?'

She introduced herself as Mary W. Clarkston, "I'm your Aunt Sissy." She was my Grandfather's sister, who drove all the way from Danbury. She squeezed my cheeks in her hands and said, "You are so beautiful. You look just like I did at your age. I absolutely loved your speech, Precious Darlin'." It made my eyes well up with tears. You are going to be fine now, because you are mine!"

She had the strong smell of Taboo, so strong a perfume that it almost knocked you down. She was adorned with pearls on her neck and ears. She was wearing a bright pink dress with pink shoes, carrying a pink purse, deep pink lipstick, and not a strand of her silver hair was out of place. She was quite thin and had the prettiest complexion of any elderly woman I had ever seen. Her eyes were like black charcoal with love seething from her tear ducts. She was rambling faster than I could keep up, as my world was already spinning from the night's events.

I took a deep breath and cut in somewhere between, 'Your Uncle Royston would have loved you,' and 'I live on Radford Avenue in Danbury,' with "So nice to meet you." My Grandmother Wells had accompanied Aunt Sissy. I had no idea they were coming, and I was surely surprised. I saw my Mother from the corner of my eye looking very uncomfortable, as they slowly approached and greeted the Wells. My Mother gave me a quick, arctic hug, and within moments, she disappeared.

I did it. In the eye of the storm, I graduated from high school, and it was my turn to prove myself, to prove I would not only survive, but excel beyond anyone's expectations. I would prove I had enough sense to get out of a "shower of s--t," to get out of Mobile, and to leave the mangled mess behind me. I knew how to work hard, and hard work became my best friend. If there was any good that Carl taught me, it was how to work diligently. He taught me how to push pass the limits of physical and mental exhaustion.

I entered Alabama Southern University a few days after my high school graduation, applying for every loan, grant, and scholarship south of the Mason-Dixon Line. I was fortunate enough to get two jobs the week I arrived, one waiting tables at the Eagles Club and the other as receptionist in Coach Ike Muller's office. I exhausted people just relaying my schedule. Classes started at 8 a.m., on to my receptionist job at noon and then to the Eagles Club at 5 p.m. I was so fortunate to earn a humble living. Eagles Club members were extremely generous with their tips, which kept my pockets full of cash.

I journeyed out of the madness one step at a time, and I created my own checklist to success. A loving husband, nice home, children, close friends, decent car, college diploma, great job...I wanted it all. I wanted to find happiness, I wanted a peaceful loving home, I dared to dream, and I dared to want what had been denied me for so long. I worked so hard to get through college and started the climb up the heap. I was a smooth blend of innocence and corruption, having only a tad of worldly experience to draw upon. I had virtually no mentoring and training on personal boundaries and relationships. My gifts were my work ethic, my art of manipulation, and my big smile. I had way too much ambition for my own good. I didn't like charity, and I wanted to be nobody's "project."

My Uncle Chip helped me purchase a late model, green Mustang for fifteen hundred dollars at a car auction, and I was able to secure a bank loan with my Grandfather Wells' signature. I had next to nothing to set up housekeeping in my 10' x 10' dorm room that I shared with a roommate. I learned the art of garage sale bargaining and quickly acquired all I needed.

My Aunt Sissy also loved to load me down every time I visited her. She lived in a modest brown brick ranch house just around the corner from campus. Her gentle nurturing soothed me. Her spunk and independence at age 70 inspired me. At quiet moments, she would squeeze my hand, lean her forehead against mine, and say, "I love you precious," and it would melt my 5-year-old heart in my 17-year-old body. Her heart of passion honored God in such an amazing way, and she encouraged me to never settle for mediocrity, to dream big, and to 'give as much love as you can.' She became my greatest cheerleader. For nearly a decade now, she has been in heaven cheering me on.

The bank funded my student loan immediately, and I walked out of that bank branch relieved. I had two thousand dollars for fall quarter tuition and was awarded the Pell Grant that paid my tuition and books. I opened a checking account and was determined to pay my bills and be financially responsible. I didn't want to repeat the financial mistakes that I witnessed in my childhood, my parents always starving for the next dollar, always extended way beyond their ability to pay. In their home, finances were a source of contention and stress that pierced the few peaceful moments.

Out of Monster Range

Now peace filled my days. No one ever yelled at me, condemned me, or exploited my dignity. No one crushed my spirit. I was free. I would sit in silence in my dorm room and relish the quiet. It was heaven. It was rare to experience volumes of silence, and I bathed in those moments. Quiet tasted sweet. Carl wasn't going to burst into my room and start hammering me on the head. No more rampages. I was alone, it was wonderfully still, and it was truly over. But in the silence, my mind would soon travel to the past. It was hard to be alone for very long, hard to quiet and still myself and not visit the painful places that seared my memory. When I was busy, I didn't have to visit those places. Busy was my friend, busy kept me sane, and busy kept me moving full-steam ahead.

CHAPTER 13

Old Friend Fear

I spot the rope, and I backstroke to it. I grab hold and am pulled to the rocks. Absolutely exhausted from the trip to the edge, this brush with death reminds me of the familiar bitter taste of my old friend Fear. What had become so familiar was yet so destructive. I hated it, yet I longed for it in a sick way. I walked in fear for so many years that it was hard to just let go. I remember the feelings of safety and deliverance. In the five minutes of struggling for my life at the bottom of that waterfall, I see my life flash in front of me, and I see how precious life is. I realize I no longer need to wake up in fear, and I no longer go to sleep in fear. I can leave that fear on this river as I leave the fear from my past in my childhood.

An instinct I believe God has designed in our minds to keep us from danger is to help us create healthy boundaries, but it kept me silenced and sentenced in my own prison. It was my prison, locked from the inside, and I owned the only key to unlock the door. With all that I have in this life and all the love that surrounds me now, how could I ever spiral so low as to want to take my own life? I don't understand how I kept silent with so much pain locked inside, and I don't ever want to lock myself in a prison of pain again.

I commit to myself and to God that I will never reach to those depths again. I will stop the downward spiral by speaking of it! Society wants silence, but I will tell; I will testify. I will prepare for the darkness and will prevent the desperation. This is the day I will commit to pray immediately when I feel the fear creep in. I commit to pull

157

out my Bible and engulf myself in scripture, for God's Word does not return void, as it says in Isaiah 55:11. "So is my Word which goes forth from my mouth: It will not return to Me empty, but will accomplish what I desire, and achieve the purpose for which I sent it." I commit to be an advocate for myself, because the little girl within needs so desperately to walk through healing. I will not be her foe but her friend. I will not condemn her for having a bad dream or letting the fear creep into the night.

I will help her walk through her anxiety with love, with prayer, and with the Word of God implanted in her heart. I will not shut her off but will share her feelings with those who love her. I will let down the armor to let others feel her pain and help her. I will let her cry and let her laugh. I will let her fail and let her enjoy her success. I will no longer punish the little girl inside. It wasn't her fault. She didn't have the power. She didn't have the tools to process what was happening to her. She couldn't tell anyone. All she had was silence and fear.

I am wearing a pair of gray athletic shorts, and I reach into my pocket thinking for sure I have lost it. I want to throw it in the river at exactly the right time in the day, but, oh well, if the river has taken it, then maybe that is the way it is meant to be. I want to release the pain and the ring at the same time. When I am ready to let go, I will know. To my surprise, it is still there. The sapphire ring is still in my pocket.

Hard Work, Hard Time

My favorite verse kept me going. "I can do all things through Christ who strengthens me." (Philippians 4:13). I started my day at 5:30 a.m.,

158

arriving at my first college class by 8 a.m. and then off to work at the coach's office at noon. Some days I could sleep until 7 a.m., if I didn't have loads of homework or a test. I loved working for Coach Muller as assistant to his full-time secretary. I made friends with everyone who walked into the office, determined to make the most of this opportunity. The coaching staff knew my plight, that I was on my own, struggling to get through college – and they were all very supportive. It was no problem to crack my textbook if I had a test or to work on homework, because they knew it would be late before my head hit my pillow.

Then it was on to the Eagles Club at 4 p.m. I would work until 10:30 p.m., Monday through Thursday and until midnight on Friday and Saturday nights. Mrs. Pitts ran the Eagles Club, and her husband Andy was the bartender. They were a sweet elderly couple who took me under their wing. It was hard work, as the kitchen was hot, and I was on my feet for hours, but I loved the smell of fried seafood. As the only waitress, I had job security. Mrs. Pitts would pitch in if I got extremely busy. No matter how hard she worked with me, she always let me keep the tips. The cream of the Danbury crop would frequent the Eagles Club, and they were all big tippers. One night I got a hundred-dollar bill. I tried to give it back, explaining that was way too generous, but they just smiled. I really insisted because I wasn't anyone's charity case.

The end of the night was the best, as Winnie the cook would fry me a huge seafood platter with the leftovers. Winnie was a heavy-set African-American woman with two gold teeth in front. We worked hard together, and I grew very fond of her. Most nights, we would eat supper together, so I never had to worry about food. She'd put her hand on mine, and every night as we would say grace, she'd say, "Child, you gonna' be just fine. God's gonna' bless ya'. You just stop that worrying, 'cuz you gonna' be just fine, you jus wait and see." Those words would stay with me through my lonely nights, through the uncertainty, through the moments of insecurity.

I would hear those words echoed a hundred times. It was as if she were my angel of encouragement. She'd recite those words every time we'd say the blessing over our fried seafood leftovers. I know she was my angel; she voiced words that gave me comfort and strength, as my heart ached with sadness. She was that mother's voice I longed to hear, and she too had her struggles. She sipped her vodka all night long, numbing the pains in her life. I not only enjoyed her company, but felt very blessed to feast on her wonderful cooking. When I was young, my mouth would water when I heard the word "shrimp." Now I feasted on fried shrimp every night.

God provided for all my needs. I always had money to pay my bills and loads of cash from tips filled my pockets. I saved. I shopped frugally at Wal-Mart and thrift stores. I was making it, and oh, how I was so proud of myself. I needed nothing from anyone. I was making it all alone. I was doing pretty well, until I met the wrong boy. He was a redneck bum that preyed on gullible freshman girls. I was a sitting duck, and he took full advantage.

Ricky was a tall, dark-haired, green-eyed smooth talker, and I fell for him hard. He was not in college and was a real loser with no morals, no ambition, just seeking a good time with a young, foolish, college babe, and I fit the bill. I was lonely, and I hung on his every word. I set myself up for big heartache. I was looking for someone or something to ease my loneliness, to ease my pain.

He filled my head with all the right words, "You are so beautiful. We'll get married as soon as you finish college. We're going to live happily ever after." I believed every word that parted his lying, scathing lips. He used my jalopy of a car to visit his girlfriend in Mississippi. He gave me every excuse in the book, and I believed every cockamamie story. He definitely gave me an education in the school of men. I gave him my all. I cooked for him, cleaned his trailer, loved him deeply, and he used me like an old Brillo pad and discarded me just as fast. I had no time to even breathe, yet broke my neck to try and make him happy. I had such a crater in my heart that I thought he could fill it. I wanted the ache to go away, and if I could find someone, anyone to love me, I thought it would ease my pain. I didn't know what love was, but I just knew I had to earn it. This is the legacy of love that I knew.

He talked me into lending him my student loan money, all that I needed for fall quarter, swearing he would pay me back within a week, long before tuition was due, so what would I have to lose? Even though I made enough money as a waitress to pay for my necessities, I still needed my student loan money to cover school expenses that the Pell Grant didn't cover.

I never, ever questioned that he would pay me back. He needed the money to fix his car, a worthy cause, and said he would pay me back with his paycheck from a pulp wood job.

He was a woodsman just like my Papa, and as it turns out, that was his only redeeming quality. I guess subconsciously I thought I could trust him, because I trusted my Papa. A few days later, I learned he quit his job and joined the Air Force. He was leaving for duty at week's end. He dumped me like a hot potato, of course, before he repaid the money. Ricky kept two steps ahead of me in the village of Danbury, not wanting to face me or his debt. My attempts at collection had failed, and I was desperate. I had to get my money back because that was the only means I had to pay for fall quarter. I didn't know who to turn to for help, and I only had twenty-four hours left.

Enemy Filters

To violated women, all men become the enemy. It is easy to use the filter of abuse to react in relationships with other men. It becomes natural to convince yourself that all men are evil and can't be trusted. Some may even go to the opposite extreme and have no boundaries when it comes to men. This is the root of many failed relationships. It takes a man of true character to love a female who has suffered sexual abuse. It takes a man who knows godly love (agape) – a love that is long-suffering, a love that lays down ego, a love that fights and never gives up. It takes a man of humility who wants to listen more than he wants to attempt to fix. It takes a patient love that is outlined in 1 Corinthians 13:6: "Love is patient, love is kind, love suffers long ... love never fails." I believe there would be similar challenges for a woman to support a sexually abused man.

God wants us to experience this kind of true love. In order to experience such love, God wants us to forgive the man who hurt us and all men who have the potential to hurt us. If we discover such a faithful man, I think that is the true meaning of a Soul Mate. I thank God I have this kind of partner as my husband, a mate who truly knows what my soul needs to heal and to be happy.

My Prince Charming

Weeks before, I had met Phillip, who was loosely introduced by Ricky as an "old friend." We bumped into him at the Backburner, a local college dance spot. Phillip was about six-feet tall; thin build, with curly blonde hair. I remember thinking to myself how cute he was the way his lips curled up on each side of his mouth. His smile was almost mischievous, but he managed to look innocent, completely harmless. I turned up the charm, if for no other reason than to make Ricky jealous. Later that evening, Phillip led me to the dance floor, and the entire time while we were dancing, he proceeded to tell me what a bum Ricky was and that he was nothing but trouble. He told me how he used every girl that crossed his path and that I looked like too nice of a girl to be wrapped up with Ricky.

Meanwhile, Ricky told me what a womanizer Phillip was, and that I needed to steer clear. Ricky and I ran into Phil a couple of times, since Danbury was a very small town. Once he was stranded on the side of the road, out of gas. We gave him a ride home, and I made a mental note of the path. Every time our eyes met, there was a spark.

So I gave up chasing Ricky for repayment and decided to solicit Phil's help. I knew Ricky was leaving the next day, and in desperation I showed up on Phil's doorstep begging for help. I explained the whole twisted story and how desperate I was to get the money back. I needed that money for my college tuition, which was now due. Phil agreed to help and told me not to worry, that he knew how to handle Ricky. I waited throughout the evening, and Phil called to let me know he had my money, no problem. I was so grateful for his help that I offered to take him to dinner, since it was all I had to offer him for his trouble. He had to work but asked for a rain check until the next Sunday.

I waited the entire week in anticipation of my benevolent dinner, and on Sunday evening, we drove to Mobile. He relayed the whole adventurous story of how he retrieved my college money, as if he were a hero in a Hollywood action film. "I knocked on the door and Ricky invited me in – supposedly just an old friend dropping in to say good-bye. As soon as I explained I was there to get your money, he got angry. I knew Ricky's temperament and expected him to turn violent. I was still standing in the doorway with my hand on the doorknob. He started to cold-cock me, so I drew the door back and hit him in the face. He fell flat to the floor, and I put my foot in his throat as I grabbed his wallet and took the money out. I showed the jerk."

To this day, I don't know how much money he was able to recover or if the story actually went down as reported, but Phil became my Superman. He returned the money and, much more than that, he gave me hope that there was someone out there to help me. I felt so alone and so betrayed. It gave me great pleasure to know that he had stuck his neck out for me.

I was enamored by his heroics and his soft, sweet charm and by the fact that I was elated to be on a date. Ricky never took me anywhere and always wanted to know what I was fixing him for dinner. This was a "real" date and Phil was acting like a perfect gentlemen. Gigolo or not, I would keep my guard up. He was cute and so very sweet, and I was drawn to him like I had never been drawn to another human being. I sensed his tender spirit. I was his damsel in distress, and he rescued me.

Ricky broke my heart. He took advantage of me. I let my need to be loved overpower my good judgment. I was so disappointed that I once again had been led into a trap of being used. I hated men now more than ever. All men disgusted me, and I felt they only wanted to use me. I knew how to use my sexuality to charm a man. I learned all too soon that I could get about anything I wanted if I played their game. It was useful, yet destructive. I felt cheap and manipulative. The very thing I detested was my weapon, and I knew it was self-destructive. I needed to change, and I wanted to change. I didn't want to be cheap; I wanted to be classy. I wanted to act like a lady; I wanted to be a lady, regardless of how my stepfather made me feel. I longed for the innocence I had never known, the innocence that was stolen by a sick man, and can never be returned. Learning to live with this reality was and is the toughest of challenges.

Even though I hated men, I really liked this Phil. I really felt a kindred spirit that I could not explain. I wanted his friendship, but I simply didn't know what a friendship could be like with a man. It mattered not what I felt, but what I had to do. I could not toy with his feelings. I could not lead him on and into a life of hurt. I knew very quickly that I must resist any emotional feelings and lock them away, for this was a no-win situation. I would either lead him into a life of confusion or down a path to which I could not commit. I was not ready to jump into another disastrous relationship. I knew I was so confused and injured that I felt I would only hurt anyone who cared for me. I was really over-thinking this simple date

All I wanted was to enjoy this evening and forget about the world, if just for the night. It began at a nice seafood restaurant, Shuckers, on River Street in Mobile. The night was heavy with humidity and emotion as we strolled along the river. We enjoyed a great seafood dinner and a few too many slow gin fizzes. I was determined to enjoy our date, keep a smile on my face as gratitude for his time and trouble, and then say goodbye. I tried to relax and be myself, a difficult task because I never let down my guard long enough to know. Unfortunately, he was forced to listen to my heartbreak-hotel stories of Ricky. We soon engaged in deeper conversation about life and love and our future dreams, conversations I had never shared with another person. My life had revolved around barely existing and merely surviving over the past few months, really over an entire lifetime, not yet daring to dream.

We began to realize that we had so much in common. He too was on his own, sending himself through college. He was raised in a dysfunctional home with a volatile father and an alcoholic mother. His mother passed away from pneumonia when he was fifteen, and his father could not afford his college education. Unfortunately, his father had been left in debt from the medical bills that had compounded through the years as he sought sobriety for his wife. Phil suffered from her substance abuse and the pain of losing her. His brother ten years his senior was completing his college education after leaving the army. They were roommates at ASU.

The late night led us to the top of the Hyatt Regency overlooking the Mobile River. A magical evening dropped a full moon overhead as we watched the cargo ships sail by, ever so slowly down the river. It was a time and a place in history that movies are made of. On the roof under the stars, the City Hall clock tower began to chime. It was 11 p.m. and we laid out the dos and don'ts of our lives and felt the stars align. The gravitational pull of our souls was beyond our control. It was an appointment with destiny as we discovered we yearned for the same life.

We both wanted what was robbed from our youth; we both longed for a happy home. When the eleventh chime echoed across the water, he looked through my eyes and stroked a lock of hair from my face as it blew in the wind. His hand cupped my face, his lips firmly pressed against my mouth, and he kissed me for what seemed like forever and a day. He kissed me long, slowly, and oh, so gently. He kissed my mouth, he kissed my lips, and he kissed my cheek ever so passionately. I melted in his arms. No one had ever kissed me with such determination, parading chills over my entire body. My head wanted to pull away, but my knees were weak and my mind was spinning. I received this tender kiss and knew that very moment that there was something stronger than my will, something stronger than I had ever felt before between us.

Was it love? Was I running to someone else to ease my pain? I saw the rockets blast and explode in my mind, and I could see in his eyes he felt the same way. We dared not speak what we felt, but only teased through the moment.

He said, "God, please throw me down a key." We were on the roof of the Hyatt Regency Hotel, and he was praying for a room key. I replied, "Sorry buddy, but I am not that easy."

It was the most romantic night of my life, and it terrified me. The fear of tangling someone else's life into the mess of mine, especially someone I cared for so quickly and so deeply, suddenly gripped me. I knew not why or how I cared for this person. We had only spent a few hours together and had brief encounters over the past three months. It was all a mystery. We curled up in a lounge chair on the roof, and he held me for a long while under the black sky with stars twinkling like diamonds overhead. I felt safe and secure snuggled under his arm, and I didn't want this precious moment to ever end. The summer breeze, the chime of the clock tower, the distant sound of the ships' horns as they slowly cruised down the river, and the kiss, were all tattooed in my memory.

We ended the night with another kiss, not quite so passionate, but it left me wanting more, with a tingle running down my spine. We made loose plans to get together again. That night I slept not a wink. I tossed and turned in my cramped dorm room bed, vowing to keep it simple and enjoy our friendship. I did not want to get hurt or cause hurt. I was on the rebound from life, and I could not see running face-first into a brick wall, a relationship that could prove to be disastrous. I could be caught up in the intense emotion of the evening. After all, I always dreamed of a fairy-tale life so far from reality. Still, I didn't really believe a fairy-tale romance was within my reach. My head would clear in the morning after a few hours of shuteye. In the morning, he may not even be interested, and he could very well become a distant memory.

The next morning I thought of nothing but the kiss. It hung on my lips like the morning dew. I felt his hand on my cheek and saw his closed eyes in my mind. I soaked the tenderness from his hands and sipped sweetness from his lips. I was daydreaming, I wanted him to hold me tight and tell me my whole life was going to be okay. I wanted a happily ever after. I could close my eyes and feel the chill bumps over my entire body with the mere thought of him.

The phone rang a couple of days later, and it was Phil. "Just wanted to say 'hi' and see how you're doing." The conversation continued for over an hour, and we made plans to see each other again. When we met, I told him all I needed was a friend right now and was not interested in anything more. He was cool, and we agreed that we would be friends. We laughed together, we cried together, and we spilled our hearts with no pressure for more. We spent many hours on the phone dissecting life and our trials, sharing our dreams and schemes. We agreed that friendship was so much more important than any short-lived romance that would end. We grew closer over the next few months, every minute revealing our true selves.

We both worked night and day and had limited leisure time. Our meetings were casual at the local bar, The Backburner, where we would scope out potential partners for each other. We would dance together and dance with other people, slyly keeping tabs on one another. Afterward, he always escorted me home, safe and sound, always with a gentleman's kiss on the cheek.

Lonely Alone

The dog days of summer were winding down, and I made it through my first quarter of college. My grades looked good, and I made lots of friends. We laughed and cried through the follies and tragedies of a co-ed dorm life. We bonded that summer. Many kids were like me, tasting freedom, total freedom, for the first time. Tragedy struck when Robin, in the dorm room just down the hall, discovered she was pregnant. She looked all of thirteen and lost her virginity on a night when she'd had too much hunch punch. This was a popular alcoholic drink that combined Kool-Aid and any available liquor. She barely knew the father and was determined to get an abortion. She insisted she could never tell her parents. I drove her to the abortion clinic because I was one of a few who had a car. Two other girls went with us. I wish I had possessed the maturity and courage to talk her out of it. I didn't, and I did what she asked: I drove. She was young, scared and naïve and thought she had no other choice. I regret driving her there. I regret not standing up for that child's right to life.

Suddenly, I was floored to learn I had to vacate my dorm room during the break between quarters. My small cell of a home was the only place I had to hang my hat. I thought, "This is a big mistake." I never dreamed I'd be evicted from my home between quarters. I knew someone would understand my plight and let me stay. I spoke to the dorm mother, my college counselor, and even went all the way to the dean, but no one had the authority to let me stay. They had a hundred excuses and rules that couldn't be broken. I couldn't hold back the tears that night for I had no place to go…I had no answers.

"All the dorms have to be professionally cleaned," was the response of one college administrator. "Our insurance won't cover you," was the response from another. "It is our policy, and can't be arbitrarily changed," was the response from a third. I went all the way to the top of the college bureaucratic ladder, and slid back down; it couldn't be overturned.
I tried to accept their answer with dignity. I tried not to cry, but I couldn't help it. I walked out of their offices blubbering like an idiot. I walked over a mile back to my dorm room trying to figure out where I would live for the next three weeks. I walked through the halls of my dorm with all the kids packing, excited

to go home. Some were talking about their families, some couldn't wait to sleep in their own bedrooms, and other co-eds shared how good their Mom's cooking was and how excited they were to anticipate waking up to the smell of French toast and bacon frying. I kept walking down the long halls to my tiny dorm room. I sat on the bed looking around at my few humble belongings, pondering how this tiny home would be taken away from me in a few days. I slowly started to pack my things in trash bags, realizing the irony that, once again, I was packing in black, plastic trash bags not knowing my destination. Once again, I felt so alone, so desperate and so very alone.

I had to be out the next day. Some friends asked me to come home with them. My friend, Samantha, said her Mom and Dad would love for me to stay with them during the break. "I can't leave my job. I have to keep working to live, to eat. Don't you understand? I have no one to depend on but myself. It is make or break-it time in my life." She looked stunned, as I continued to scream at her in my despair. Though she tried to relate, she had no clue about my reality. She had a big, fat college fund from her grandparents and open arms waiting for her at home.

I was jealous. Everyone, it seemed, had helping parents but me, and as I saw the benefits of their parents, it made me think of the abuse and abandonment from my parents. My classmates were blessed; I was cursed. I tried so hard not to hate them all.

I knew of no other student in my shoes - no one who struggled on their own but me - and my strength was waning. They say struggle is nature's way of making you stronger. Well, at the age of eighteen, by that standard, I should have felt like an ox. There were days when I had to be stronger than I looked, when I had to let the strife roll off me like the rain. And that's what I did. It was a dog-day summer afternoon thunderstorm and the bottom fell out. I stood outside in the rain and let the pain roll down my body with each raindrop that hit me.

It felt good to cry. I looked to the heavens and screamed as the lightening danced around me and the clapping thunder made my heart jump. I let go in the parking lot without anyone around to watch my self-contained meltdown. Soaked to the bone and shivering with emotion, I made my way back inside. I didn't want anyone's pity, so I dried my eyes and put my smile back on.

The hot-pink posters slapped me in the face. Plastered on all the exit doors, they notified students to be out by 6 p.m. It was 5:45 p.m. on Sunday when I packed the last trash bag in my car. Everything I owned fit in that green Mustang packed to the brim; I was the last car to drive out of the parking lot. So I swallowed my salty tears, as I had nowhere to go. My car became my home for the next three weeks. I paid for a hotel room one night, but I couldn't afford fifty-nine dollars a night for the next twenty-one days. I didn't know the Wells well enough, although I'm sure I would have been welcome to stay with them, and I did crash in their motor home a few nights. I couldn't go home, God forbid; it had taken so much courage to leave. I didn't have enough gas money to drive all the way to Mobile every day to stay with my Aunt. I bounced here and there, took spit baths in service station bathrooms, stuffed my pocket book with left over baked potatoes from the Eagles Club, slept in my car and survived the three weeks. It was an eternity.

As Scarlett vowed to never be hungry again, I vowed to never be homeless again. I prayed so hard for a permanent home. I put a plan in motion to get an apartment and truly make a permanent home for myself. I couldn't take the pain of feeling like such an outcast. I needed roots, if only sprigs; I needed security. I had experienced enough flux in my life, and I now needed a constant, a place to call home.

It wasn't easy, but I started my campaign to get the dean of the college to waive the rule that freshmen could not live off campus. I was determined to have a home by Christmas. As it turns out, God's timing is always perfect. A few days before Thanksgiving, I received a letter from the dean asking to meet with me. When I met with him, he granted the waiver for the winter quarter. I got the bright idea to get Mrs. Pitts from the Eagles Club to talk to her friend about renting an apartment I could afford. Mrs. Pitts knew everybody in town and was eager to help me.

She helped me find a furnished apartment, and I negotiated the rent down to $375 per month. And to make life even easier, I now had a roommate who was willing to move into the apartment with me and share the rent and living expenses. I couldn't have been happier; I was going to have my own home by the time the dorms emptied. I would drive away to my new apartment. I praised God. I was going to have a home for Christmas, and that was the best gift ever.

CHAPTER 14

Over the Cliff

A couple of other successful runs keep me safely in the raft, and now it is time to pull out of the river for a lunch break. A huge cliff towers over our lunch spot. A group of young girls half my age starts up the cliff and encourages me to join them. I have always been afraid of heights and quickly decline the offer. They will not take "no" for an answer.

They ask me, "When was the last time you dove off a 40-foot cliff?"

"I've never taken a leap like that, and I'm scared to death of heights."

They laugh and continue to taunt me. Up they climb, yelling my name from above. "Angie, don't be a chicken!" Off flies the first girl, with spread arms and straight legs, then moving her arms down, she executes a perfect swan dive, just like a pro. Then the next goes feet first and another flails, giggling all the way. "Chicken, chicken, chicken," their screams echo off the cliff. I can stand their taunting no more. Do or die, I am taking the plunge.

Up the cliff I climb, clinching each rock, hand over foot, as fast as I can before I lose my nerve. At the top, I peer down into the black water. It takes me back to another time, determined to end my life, when I peered down into a black abyss from the bridge over the Mobile Bay, petrified. My stomach is in my throat, and the chants are ringing in my ear.

"Jump, Jump, Jump, Jump." Today I will jump to live life to its fullest.

I close my eyes tight and jump out as far as I can. I don't have the nerve to attempt a dive. I'm not a chicken, but I look like one, arms flailing as everyone witnesses my lack of coordination. I drop like a rock, and when I hit, I smile, feeling the burn of the water on my body. The crowd is applauding loudly. I survive yet another adventure on the river.

I reach into my pocket, and surprisingly the sapphire ring is still there. I take it out and start to climb back up the cliff to throw it in the river. Something tells me to put it back in my pocket. It isn't time.

Falling Fast

It was late October, and my college career had lasted a whole five months. I was finally in a groove with work, classes, and a budding relationship. There was a nip in the night air when Phil and I had a date at a fraternity party after work. There was plenty of beer and plenty of obnoxiously drunk college students. It was Friday night, way past midnight, and we were both exhausted from the day's classes and work. In the midst of the college crowd, we warmed ourselves around a bonfire. On into the night, the music blared. Phil stood behind me, and I leaned my head back against his chest in exhaustion. I felt his arms slither around my waist. I felt his breath on my neck and heard his soft, low voice, as he began to softly sing along to the Rolling Stones…

"Let me whisper in your ear
Angie, Angie, where will it lead us from here?
Oh, Angie, don't you weep,
All your kisses still taste sweet
I hate the sadness in your eyes…"

I felt a tremble through my body to my feet.

I couldn't let him fall in love with me, because he deserved so much more. He deserved a life partner who didn't come with so much baggage. I couldn't make him happy. I can't make me happy. I can't even make it through a night without scorching nightmares. The words circled inside my head as I thought silently, "Please don't sing in my ear, please don't make me feel so safe, please don't fall in love with me. Please, let us just be friends forever. I don't want this to get complicated."

His arms were strong, and warmed my chilled body. I broke the embrace just as the song ended. "Do you mind walking me back to my dorm? I am so tired," I pleaded. It had been months since we last kissed, and I longed for the taste of his lips. We walked through the frigid night with his arm around my neck and arrived at my dorm door. I leaned against the wall to say goodnight, and he put his hands on either side above my head, pinning me against the brick wall. My eyes were saying goodnight, but my lips were saying, "Kiss me." He touched my lips tenderly with his index finger, slowly outlining their shape. Then he leaned into me, closed his eyes, and kissed me like tomorrow would never come. It was a long, passionate kiss that took me to the ring of Saturn. He looked deep into my eyes and whispered, "Angie, I didn't mean to … but I fell in love with you."

I looked up at him sadly and said, "You can't." With that, I raced inside my dorm room and locked the door. I stood there holding the doorknob with my forehead pressed against the cold metal door. My heart raced and my hands were sweaty. His words circled my mind like a Ferris wheel … "I fell in love with you."

My mind raced as I thought, "I can't love you. I don't know how to love you. I don't even love myself. Please God, please make him go away and never think of me again. Please God, I don't want to hurt him, and I can't begin to tell him the torture I've been through. He wouldn't even want me if he knew the truth. No one will want me if they know my past, no one."

For days, I didn't answer the phone. I couldn't respond, and I in no way wanted to hurt him. I prayed in time he would just disappear and find someone else to love. Not me, I wasn't the one. He was persistent. Every day he called. We bumped into each other on campus. He asked if we could just talk. He apologized for rushing me and said we could just remain friends, but that he needed to see me. Finally, I agreed.

We had so much fun together that it was difficult for either of us to make it through the day without seeing the other. We had no money, so we had to make our own fun. We would go fishing in a flat-bottom boat at my Grandfather Wells' farm. Eating way too many platters of fried shrimp, I was putting on weight like crazy. Oddly, the weight felt good. It was an insulator to the pain, and the food a comforter to the loneliness and the silent suffering.

One fishing trip, we stepped in the boat on opposite ends, and I lifted his end of the boat up, out of the water. I could either laugh or cry from embarrassment. We laughed until we cried. There was no condemnation in his eyes, no judgment in his

179

reaction. He accepted me just like I was. I had listened to Carl call my Mother a "fat pig" for years. I now knew what it was like to feel overweight, and I feared Phil thought I was fat.

We fell into a love so deep we could hardly breathe apart. He wanted me more than he could express. I led him down a path of deceit, as if I had no experience in that department. I didn't want him to know about my past, about the abuse I had suffered, about the promiscuous relationships I had entertained. I wanted to be innocent. I wanted to reinvent myself for him. I wanted to be someone else, someone who didn't come with so much baggage and shame. I never spoke of it, but somehow he knew. He knew there was a cavernous throbbing in my eyes and shrapnel in my heart. He knew the canvas was complex. He knew something terrible had happened to me, and he knew I didn't want to share. We played cat and mouse for many weeks until the tension became volcanic.

He didn't wait for me. He went out with another girl, and I was heartbroken. I ran into him at a bar where he liked to shoot pool, and there she was - a cute, short blonde hanging all over him with her arms clenched around his neck. I confronted him, and he didn't lie. He introduced her as his girlfriend. I immediately made a beeline to the ladies room, and he followed me alone. He saw the hurt in my eyes, and I could hear the frustration in his voice, "I've been very honest about my feelings for you, and you ignore them. I laid my heart on the line, and you didn't act interested. What do you expect me to do, keep waiting?" I shook my head and found the exit.

Phil with someone else ... I was so hurt. But why should I be hurt? I told him for months I only wanted friendship. What did I expect from him, that he would wait forever, that he would never lay eyes on another girl, especially one who was pursuing him with such aggression? At that moment, I had to decide whether to take a leap of faith or walk away. I couldn't keep him on a leash any longer. I had to love him or let him go. I decided to figure out how to love him. If I walked away, I knew I would never walk back. It was a great decision.

CHAPTER 15

Laying New Foundations

My ongoing struggles were working my way through college and trying to build a lasting relationship. I sought wisdom from people I respected, and all too often, I wound up on Aunt Sissy's doorstep. She always greeted me with warm hugs and kisses, which I craved. She showered me with the sweet nurturing I never experienced before. Her cozy home swayed at a slow, easy pace. I would join her in one of her chenille lazy boy recliners to catch the end of the Braves game or interrupt her pouring through the daily news. We would talk for the few minutes I had between classes or shift change. It was a step off of my rat wheel.

Aunt Sissy was a healthy, normal, and good influence. I would hear about her life and the enormous tragedy that plagued it. She lived a fairy tale existence with love and laughter, and yet suffered through great sorrow. She lost her parents, her brother and, in the prime of her life, both her son and her husband, who was her soul mate. Yet, she always smiled and carried a joy in her heart that was infectious. She was delightful, and I enjoyed the time we spent together. For that moment in time, she filled my life with her joy, love and wisdom.

When I met her, she was approaching seventy. She taught me her secrets to happiness. Her habits were foreign to me. She started her day with exercise, with a Word from God, spreading her Bible open at breakfast with the discipline of devotion and prayer.

She ate well, she rested well, and she took time to enjoy life. Every meal was eaten on China plates, crystal glasses, matching cloth napkins and placemats, flowers and a candle. She always began with a blessing. She chewed slowly and deliberately, like she chewed life. She embraced life with a colossal spirit and took each day with a grain of salt.

We were good for each other because she could talk for hours about her precious husband and the love they shared. She also could reclaim the memories of her son whom she had adopted as a baby, since she was never able to bear children. The memories took her to the end of each life. Donnie was shot in the heart while hunting at age thirteen. He actually died in her arms on the way to the hospital. The shot, the car, the clothes she was wearing, she would recount every detail as the tears rolled down her thin, lightly wrinkled cheeks. Though it was immense torture, she needed to talk about her pain. It was all new to me, so I hung on to her every word. I learned so much from her, and I soaked in her unconditional love. It felt so good to feel her love, to feel her arms around me, to feel her hand in my hand; her love was like a soothing ointment to my wounds.

Aunt Sissy continued to tell me the valleys she had walked through with Jesus by her side. A few years after her son passed away, her husband died of a heart attack. They had been her whole life, and she learned to go on after the pain. Her loss was enormous. She taught me so much about how I could go on after my pain. She taught me about a love I had never known, a love I had never witnessed. She taught me so much about relationships. She preached forgiveness, not for others, but for me. She taught me how to forgive myself and live my life without excuses or sorrow. She taught me to seek God's favor in all my doings and to be content with what each day brings. She taught me to be responsible for my happiness.

From time to time, whenever I want to remember Aunt Sissy, I pull her golden cameo fragrance case of Avon Taboo from my jewelry case and breathe in her signature perfume. I can still close my eyes feel her warm hugs and hear her famous words, "Precious," as she often referred to me, and sayings like "Life is so funny as it unfolds, Darlin'." Aunt Sissy was so proud of my every triumph. She loved me unconditionally and made me feel precious for the first time in my life. Her spirit lives with me always.

Going Back Free

I worked hard to keep all the balls in the air: school, work, Phil, Aunt Sissy, developing relationships with the Wells family, reconnecting with my Mother, and burying my childhood. Believe me when I say, it was emotionally draining juggling act that stretched me very thin. Phil soon became my priority. I wanted to spend every waking moment with him. He filled my every thought, and I lived through each day for the moment our eyes would meet. We spent hours on the phone and hours learning every detail about each other. We would spend hours studying together. Some days it didn't matter what we were doing, as long as we were together. Those were some of the best times: holding hands on the couch watching old movies. We lived on short sleep, less money, and lots of love. We would talk for hours on end about what we wanted from life and what we wanted from each other.

He showed such tenderness for months with a patience to absorb what I was able to share. One magical night I realized God had introduced me to my soul mate and, most of all, I knew I loved him more than life itself. Then I began to unravel the secret and tell him what I thought he was able to digest. He listened intently. He would get angry, totally disgusted with my disclosure. In a few days, he would meet Carl. He would try to swallow the fact that he would have to be civil and respond in a way that would keep the door open for me to stay in touch with my sisters. I had to make him understand how important that was to me, much more important than any vindication he could slice out of the situation. I painted the picture of how terrible the whole ordeal would be and how important it was that he plays along with the lie; that he put up a front with me.

I really didn't want to introduce Phillip to my family. I cringed at the thought of him meeting Carl, at experiencing my Mother's desperation, and at walking into such volatility. I couldn't control what we were about to face, and a part of me was scared that he would take two seconds to decide to get the heck out of Dodge and out of my misfit world.

We spent Thanksgiving at 465 Briar Patch Place with a nice dinner and made small talk around the turkey. Carl even acted as though he were quizzing Phil as my prospective mate. How sick was that? We survived the stress of the visit, and Phil, for the first time, got a glimpse into my past, my dysfunction. He saw the weakness in my Mother and the power Carl had over her and over 465 Briar Patch Place. It felt really good that he no longer held power over me.

It didn't take much for me to make Carl angry, and I did it. I crawled in bed with Phil – in the front guest bedroom, of course. I wasn't about to leave Phil's side, because he would protect me. I acted brave under his arm, but I shook in fear every time I entered 465 Briar Patch Place. Carl went ballistic because he no longer had control over me because I was with another man; I was breaking all his rules by "shacking up." We could hear him screaming and cursing from the other end of the house, his master bedroom. I had to hold Phil down and told him we'd leave early in the morning. Phil was ready to jump out of bed and start swinging. Phil was ready to protect my honor; Phil was ready to kill him. He had no idea how cruel Carl was, but I knew that, like he often did when he was threatened, Carl would go for his gun. I had to hold Phil down with all of my power, because I had no doubt, Carl would kill him, and then plead self-defense.

I could see the bloody horror flash before me. I told Phil, "We can either leave or lie, but you are not going to confront him now in the middle of his rage." Within minutes, Phil understood me and my life of abuse. Of course, sugar wouldn't melt in his mouth the next morning, for deep down, Carl was a coward. Phil hated him and felt the evil force that possessed him and paralyzed me. We drove away from 465 Briar Patch Place and away from the evil that resided there.

We traveled on to Eufaula to meet Phil's family, a seemingly peaceful home in contrast to 465 Briar Patch Place. They lived in a white clapboard house in the middle of town, with very modest décor, explaining Phil's frugal nature. His Daddy was a sweet, elderly man with deep lines etched in his face from years of troubles. His stepmother was gracious, but cautious. He was raised in a small rural town that had "hello" and "goodbye" on the welcome sign. His whole family joined us for a Thanksgiving supper, and I met the stepbrothers, as well as Phil's brother again. That night, Phil was fixing his bed on the couch and led me to the one extra bedroom. Phil's father asked, "Is this the way you sleep at home?" We both blushed, and he told Phil to "get to bed." Phil's daddy adored me, and I adored him from the moment I laid eyes on him. We shared a common interest – Phil's happiness.

The Coat of Forgiveness

Christmas was a precious time. We drove to Dothan to welcome my new half-brother into this world. Though I kept my distance from my biological father, I was trying so hard to connect to this new family, and it was very difficult. The Wells seemed distant, and I kept my walls up, because I didn't want any more pain in my life. Not now. The whole drive there, I tried not to focus on the fact that Norbert walked away from me as a baby, yet today he was bringing another baby into the world. My real father was so void of emotion; he was like a glacier. It was easy to keep them at bay, because they were not the most loving family, with the exception of Aunt Sissy, of course.

I didn't have a coat, and it was freezing. Phil pulled into a mall and bought me a rabbit fur coat. It had so much more meaning than he ever realized, and that coat still hangs in my closet. It reminds me of what his love did for me. Love gave me warmth, love covered the coldness in my heart, and love was a soft touch and protected me from the bitterness and despair that I had wallowed in for so many years.

Phil knew. He knew what I told him, and he knew what I neglected to tell him. In the beginning of our developing relationship, I never went too deep, because I really wanted to put my past behind me. I was finally beginning to smile more than I cried. I was beginning to see a future. And then he broke the news: he'd be graduating in June and moving to Birmingham to get a good job. That was a hard blow. He was leaving me.

He didn't actually walk in graduation until the beginning of June. The months we'd spent together seemed so brief. He fed me all the right lines, "We'll keep in touch. I'll call you every day. I'll come back to Danbury, and you can visit me in Birmingham. It'll be fine, and we'll stay close." He said he loved me. I had to believe him; I had no choice now, I loved him, I needed him.

We traveled back and forth as frequently as possible. I'll never forget my nineteenth birthday. I went to Birmingham to visit him, and we spent a fun day at Alabama Adventure and had a wonderful romantic dinner that night. We made passionate love, and he lit nineteen matches for me to blow out for my birthday wish. I wished I could be in his arms for a lifetime.

I tried desperately to learn to live without Phil, but I couldn't. I knew he was in Birmingham living without me. This time apart gave me time to dwell on my past; I slid back. The anger fueled me, and I was determined to get revenge. I was so furious that Carl made me out to be a liar. I was so demoralized every time I visited and had to face him and my Mother. He would snidely laugh, like he was the nicest man in the world. I knew now time was passing, and he had passed his "parole period" with my Mother. He had exhibited his best behavior after I left, fearing the other shoe would drop. I think he truly feared I would have the courage to prosecute him for his crime. But now his harshness toward her had returned. I could see it in my Mother's face. I listened as my sisters recapped his rampages. I could get in my green Mustang and drive away, but they had to stay, and that hurt me deeply. I had to face the lies, and my strength was waning. I decided I would take matters into my own hands.

I devised a master plan. I would have a gun in one pocket and a tape recorder in the other. I would show up when he was home alone. He would without a doubt rape me, and I would kill him in self-defense. I would have proof on the recorder and be vindicated. Praise God, the pawnshop wouldn't sell me a gun. My life could have taken a grave turn. But I still got joy playing out the scene in my head. I wanted him to pay. I began to pray to God that he would pay. But somewhere inside, I knew I had to quit obsessing over his demise. The rage was festering inside me and was infesting my life. I wanted Carl out of my life, but I knew I didn't have the power. Finally, I turned him over to God and tried desperately to trust that God is a God of justice, as I believed, a God who would redeem my pain and take the responsibility out of my hands. I could hear God calling me, but I had a long way to go on my own before I would answer His call.

With Phil gone, the loneliness set in. I felt he didn't want me, because he had left. I knew, logically, that he was in search of his dream, the dream of a good job that would defy the poverty in which he had been reared. He was in search of himself, and I felt I was only a detour in his path. What could I offer him but strife?

We attempted a long-distance relationship that produced unfaithfulness. I needed him more than he could ever dream. I needed arms around me daily, and I needed to know I mattered to someone. Every day, I slipped into not mattering. We would talk as long as we thought we could pay the long distance phone bill and hang up, then call each other again the next hour. We would make swift trips from city to city, a four-hour drive, just to hold each other. We knew we belonged together but neither of us was strong enough to make the commitment. It wasn't enough, and in my weakness, I cheated on him. It all started very innocently with an evening study session with a fellow classmate, a friend, a good-looking male friend. The early evening was innocent, and then the kidding started and, before I knew it, I had been unfaithful to Phil. In a moment of weakness, I had proven myself unworthy of his love. There was no love involved in my infidelity, no tenderness, only the feeling of shame that I was left with every time Carl finished with me. I tried not to vomit, but dressed quickly, told him it was a big mistake, and made a run for the door. That night I screamed in pain. I had blown the one shot I had for happiness. I had destroyed a trust between us, between Phil and me. I did it. I ruined it. It was all my fault and I had to face Phil as a failure. I now had another secret, and I was the queen of keeping a secret. I would pretend nothing happened, and it would go away. Not so easy. Every phone conversation was strained, every word contrived. Every time I spoke to him, I knew I had to tell him and face the consequences. I betrayed his trust, I knew Phil would be furious, and I knew it would be over. He is a man of his word and a man of integrity. I would speak the words, and it would be over. I knew if he saw my face, he would see the betrayal in my eyes.

It was Friday night, and I begged off from work. I baked some brownies, why I don't know, but I thought he would see through this small act, how much I loved him. It was a long, four-hour drive to Birmingham. Every mile I drove, I beat myself. I dreaded the night to come. I didn't even know if I was capable of honesty. I considered that I might be on the road back to Danbury tonight. I owed him honesty, I owed him the truth about everything in my life, and I would leave him knowing we were not meant to be.

He answered the door, and we embraced. I hated myself more in that moment than ever, and I hated the monster I had let Carl create in me. He knew immediately that there was something very, very wrong. I wasn't ready for the words to depart my lips. I so wanted one more hour with him. I brushed him off with, "There's nothing wrong. I'm very tired." There was a party at the pool that we joined, and I focused on soaking him in, knowing every word to me may be his last. I knew at that moment I wanted him more than life itself. I loved him more than I could put into words, and I had to tell him this and walk out of his life. Later that night, we sat on the sofa in his apartment and listened to jazz. As he stroked my hair, I was lost in the peace. I had no choice. I could belabor it no more. I couldn't look in his eyes. I spit out the words. "I've betrayed you. I've been with another guy."

He was furious; the words crushed him. Tears flooded down his face, and the hurt indicted me. I was ready to run now, "I'm going, and I am so very sorry I hurt you. I'm driving back to Danbury tonight, and I'll be out of your life for good. You don't deserve this."

He looked up, "No, don't go." He wouldn't let me leave. I don't think he wanted me to stay, but he also didn't want me to leave. I tried to explain, but there was no explanation. I think he knew if I left, he would never see me again. I told him: "I am just a bad person. I am toxic, and you should want no part of me. I have no answers. I have no right to be in your life. And maybe one day we can find the precious friendship we had in the beginning of our relationship." The silence seemed to last forever, as he walked down to the pool at his apartment complex and left me alone. He said he needed some time to think. I waited. I sat there in the dark, wanting to claw my face, wanting to dig all the ugliness out of me. I could scrape layers off my face and never reach the shame. At that moment, I found no redeeming quality in myself. There was a paralyzing silence when he returned. I collapsed in his arms. He held me through my weeping, and I'll always remember his words: "I can't believe you cheated on me. I hate what you did to me, but I don't hate you. I'm hurt, but I'm going to try to forgive you, because I love you Angie. Then a long silence hung in the room. "You mean everything to me."

He wouldn't let me leave. I tried to sleep on the floor on a quilt to give him his space. He curled up behind me on the floor, and we lay there in the dark holding each other and crying. His arms were like a cast to my wounded soul. Gradually, every day got better, and healing came to our fragile union. He forgave me. We spent months apart and somehow that painful mark on our relationship made us stronger. He did the unexpected: he did not give up on me. Somehow, overnight, our love grew to a deeper level. Throughout this time, I really didn't love myself, and I felt so unlovable. I don't know how we got through it, but we did, and I thank God. Phil loved me through my mistakes.

CHAPTER 16

The Lightning Bolt of Love

It was the happiest phone call I ever received. Phil and I had been spending many hours on the phone planning our future. We were planning a life of happiness together. We ached to be together, side by side, and it was tough trying to love long-distance. We longed to hear each other's voice every day, to feel each other's touch. Then came that call: "Let's get engaged," he said. "Come to Birmingham, and let's get engaged."

I went. Well, he didn't drop to his knees with a ring box in his hand as I had imagined, but it was a solid commitment and a wonderful invitation into his life and into his future. That was enough for me because I was so tired of being alone and so tired of fighting my battles by myself. Alone was exhausting, but with him, he gave me strength.

The next weekend, he arrived with a tiny diamond ring enclosed in a small black velvet box. With no job and living with his uncle, striving to get his start in this rigid big city world, this precious ring was all he could afford. It didn't matter if it was retrieved from a Crackerjack box, that ring meant the world to me. It meant that someone finally loved me more than he loved himself. It meant that maybe, just maybe, I would have a chance at happiness. I had no idea the God of the universe had chosen the perfect soul mate for me. He placed a faithful man in my life that would stand in the gap for me through my darkest days and love me passionately and sacrificially.

That June, Phil returned for graduation from Alabama Southern College, and I was so very proud of him. He received a college education, and now he had a job with a Fortune 500 company. He returned for the formality of donning the cap and gown and walking down to receive his college diploma, the first in his immediate family to have done so. We gathered that evening with family and friends to celebrate his success, and I was one proud, young girl to be on his arm. We were so happy. We grinned at each other at every glance.

I put plans in motion to move to Birmingham. I didn't own much, so the move was simple. I transferred my college credits to Alabama State University and made a contact in Birmingham with the manager of a dress shop in NorthPoint Mall. She hired me immediately. We couldn't afford an apartment alone, so we shared a place with one of Phil's old roommates, Hank, a notorious character. He had an ego the size of Texas, great looks, and such arrogance. He was a Marine serving in the reserves and always had a grenade or two to launch. His GI-Joe persona played into his every move. I couldn't stand sharing our tiny apartment and counted the days when we would both be on our feet and able to get our own place. We were off to a rocky start between our living arrangements and the stress I was under with full-time school and a full-time work schedule. We stole time alone when Hank had to go to Army reserve training one weekend a month. Hank soon had a girlfriend, Mendy, who monopolized a lot of his time, leaving one-on-one time for Phil and me.

I had never been a stranger to hard work and that didn't change when I got to Birmingham. I had to work hard to keep up in school and to make a living. Phil and I split expenses, and of course, I wanted to pull my weight.

I was nearing the end of my college career. Praise God it had been a long, arduous task to receive my four-year degree in three years. I was succeeding at the dress shop and had attained top saleswoman three months in a row. It was time for my review, and I'll never forget the meeting. I got accolades, praises, and a nickel an hour raise. I was making minimum wage at three dollars and fifteen cents an hour at the time, and a nickel an hour enraged me. I walked out and never returned. I decided I needed to get a good job that was within 5 blocks of Alabama State University, the maximum distance I determined I could comfortably walk to school in the evening. The next day I went to the top of the Southern Bank Building. I had landed a job as a receptionist for a law firm when I was sixteen, and worked a short time in Nicole's Dad's law firm, which gave me some experience and confidence. I also had a knack to typing and could spit out 100 words a minute. Now with more maturity and business sense, I knew I could get a good job in an office.

The Southern Bank building had twelve floors, and I started at the top and worked my way down. In and out of each office I went asking, "Are you looking for any help? Is your company hiring?" The "no's" slapped me in the face a dozen times, but I kept on trying. I made it to the eighth floor and walked into Willis, Dodgen & Johnston, a real estate consulting

196

and development firm. The lady at the front desk seemed more than overwhelmed, as the phones were ringing, files were stacked sky high, and dirty coffee cups were scattered around. I immediately saw opportunity.

I barely got the words out of my mouth when she said "Yes, but Mr. Willis is in a meeting." I said, "That'll be just fine, I'll be happy to wait." She said, "It may be hours." I replied, "That'll be fine, I can wait all afternoon, because I can't go home without a job."

While I waited, I began to wash coffee cups. I offered to help with filing, and in the second hour, she showed me how to answer the phone. When Mr. Willis broke from his meeting hours later, he walked into the reception room to find me already working. I introduced myself and said I desperately needed a job. I was hired on the spot, and that was the birth of a twenty-year real estate career. I was able to work until 5 p.m. and finish my college degree at night. Those were long days, but this time in my life was a turning point for me in many ways. I was promoted quickly and gained an enormous amount of experience. I earned a good salary for my age and started pressing Phil for a wedding date. I was never truly comfortable with cohabitation and didn't have the backbone to give him "the" ultimatum. He was determined that he wanted me to finish college before we married. Many nights I would come home from school to find a hot bath drawn. He was always available to quiz me or help with any project. He was my biggest cheerleader, and when times got really tough, his cheers kept me trudging onward.

Throughout all of this, my Aunt Sissy remained a constant source of encouragement and love in my life. We grew very close, and she gave me an incredible college graduation gift. She invited me to accompany her to Greece for a two-week excursion. We had the time of our lives, and it opened my eyes to a big world I knew nothing about. While we were away, a TWA flight was hi-jacked out of Athens, Greece. Phil was back in the U.S. worried sick that I may have been on that flight. I had left him with no definite travel plans, and he worried for days until I finally called from Athens. We knew nothing of the hijacking. I called because I missed him desperately and couldn't wait another moment to hear his voice.

The first words out of his mouth were, "What will it take for you to never leave me again?"

"I guess you'll have to marry me," I replied.

Phil answered, "Marry me when you get back. Marry me now. I love you, and I don't want to spend a day without you."

The long-distance call from Greece cost a fortune, and I hung up the phone telling him I would marry him as soon as I got home. I returned in June, but I was so sure of our union, that I purchased our wedding bands while I was in Turkey – two thin 18-karat gold wedding bands that had a diamond cut design in the gold. We married on August 31st, Labor Day Weekend. We've worn them now since the mid-'80s and haven't taken them off for more than an hour. He met me at the top of the escalator at Birmingham International Airport with a tear in his eye, bent on one knee, a giant elated smile on his face, and a huge bouquet of red roses in his hand. My heart exploded with joy.

The night before we were married, we kneeled before Aunt Sissy, and she prayed over us. She prayed for joy, peace, happiness, and a love that would grow stronger through the storms of life. I felt the Holy Spirit in the room. I knew this was God's ordained will for my life. I dressed in a Sunday School classroom into a pretty white satin and lace dress that I purchased at a second hand store. I put on my long, white, sheer veil and looked in the mirror.

I remember the overwhelming feeling of being special. For a moment, I felt pure and innocent. That was my wedding gift from God. We stood before God and a small gathering at First Woodlawn Methodist Church in Danbury, Alabama, and said our vows on August 31, 1985. When I heard our song playing, "Looking through the Eyes of Love," I wanted to run down the aisle toward Phil. When the doors opened, I adorned my Grandfather Wells' arm, and couldn't race down the aisle fast enough to become Phil's life partner, his wife till death do we part.

This day changed the course of my life for eternity. It was a simple ceremony with a reception of punch and cake in the church fellowship hall. It was the first time I ever witnessed my Mother and my biological father in the same room. Carl chose not to attend, but allowed my Mother to participate in the wedding ceremony. Phil and I were married, and that was, and is, all that mattered.

The Thursday before I left for my wedding, I informed my boss that I would be back on Monday. He inquired about our honeymoon plans, and I told him we could barely afford the small wedding that Phil and I paid for and that we planned to spend the night in Mobile at the Hyatt, returning to work on Monday. That afternoon before I left, I went to the restroom. When I returned to my desk, I found two tickets to Jamaica for a one week, all-inclusive stay at a Jamaica resort. No words can express my gratitude.

We had the time of our lives. The ocean meets the mountains in Jamaica, a land of beauty. I saw Phil in the rock and in the mountain, and I was the ocean. Like the waves, I churned inside, and like the mountain, Phil stood steady and firm. As I crashed against him, he welcomed me back time and time again. Sometimes, the waves crushed him, and sometimes, the waves gave him great joy. I didn't feel as though I deserved any of the heaping helping of happiness I was served in this moment. I certainly drank it all in, thinking it would be fleeting, betting on it ending. As much as I wanted the 'happily ever after', I was so afraid of it. Feeling good felt so foreign, and feeling that someone loved me beyond himself felt unimaginable. As we walked along the long white sandy beaches under a million twinkling stars, we imagined a happily ever after with no clue what lay ahead, but knowing deep down our love would always survive.

But the survival tactics that I learned while captive to Carl had become obsessive behaviors in my adulthood. I was a party girl. It became so easy to abuse drugs and alcohol to avoid dealing with the memories of Carl that seemed to lurk around so many normal activities. The drugs and the alcohol became an anesthetic. Maybe it was rebellion against the strict authority of my home life. I was taught a Southern Baptist didn't dance or drink. Yet I didn't trust myself enough to be accepted without the influence.

Phil soon gathered that life with Angie would be an adventure. I was the life of the party and fought to be the center of attention. By sheer coincidence, while in Jamaica, we met a couple from a town close to Phil's small hometown. We bonded with them immediately and had a blast exploring Jamaica.

Phil decided to go scuba diving for the first time, and I parked by the pool ordering one mud slide after another. Sheila, my newfound friend, joined me in my mischief, and once we were good and tanked, we were convinced we must take up sailing.

A Jamaican who ran the all-inclusive activities arranged our excursion. We jumped in the sailboat without fear or hesitation. Off we went on a sailing adventure. We were headed out to sea, destined for the nude beach, the James Bond Beach, on a catamaran captained by our newfound Jamaican friend. We were young, stupid, and absolutely invincible. We were laughing and joking, and then he asked if we were going to lose our swimsuits when we got there. That shocked us back into reality and sobered us fast. We said "absolutely not," and reality started to set in. We were in the middle of the ocean, with the shore getting farther and farther away in a foreign country, with a total stranger. We both acknowledged our fear as Sheila's and my eyes met, wide and scared.

Within minutes, we were literally in over our heads. We were both gasping for air and sputtering and spitting water. The boat capsized on a reef and the sail was holding us both under water. We struggled out from under the sail to realize neither of us had on a life jacket, and I was a weak swimmer. Our guide was off rescuing the sailboat, and we were left to sink or swim. I tried to remember the swimming lessons Phil had given me and tried desperately not to remember the time I almost drowned in twelve feet of water once when I got a leg cramp. I kicked and waved my arms back and forth and spotted Sheila, doing a smooth and steady backstroke, but going in the wrong direction, swimming out to sea, away from shore. I could see land in the distance and screamed for her to turn around. She was in panic mode, and I was not far behind.

We caught up to each other and started our fight to shore. Jellyfish swarmed around us and attacked Sheila. Her shrieks of pain terrified me as my kicking legs whipped across the razor sharp coral reef. Blood stained the clear blue water as all I could think is, "We're shark meat, dead shark meat."

I screamed, "Sheila, swim, just swim, swim fast! Close your eyes and swim!"

Within minutes, we spotted these massive, muscular Rastafarians with long dreadlocks swimming toward us. They scooped us up and began running to shore. We were both terrified, and all we could do is laugh hysterically. God only knew where they were taking us, and we could do absolutely nothing. They looked so scary in their Speedos, and we were a mess, hyperventilating – cut, stung and scared. Down the beach they ran, carrying us like in a Tarzan movie.

They kept shouting, "You good lady, no problem. No problem!" Then in the distance, we spotted the gate to our resort, and it looked like the gates to heaven. They carried us to the infirmary on the resort and left us there to be treated. We were in shock, as they bandaged and wrapped our wounds. We recounted the whole adventure, stunned that we had survived. We were fortunate and finally able to exhale. We both said at the same time, "We need a drink."

Off to the bar we ran, when from behind, in the distance, I heard Phil yelling, "Angie!", then louder, "ANGIE!" I kept walking, faster, and faster, and faster. He kept yelling, so I looked over at Sheila and said, "I have to turn around."

When we turned, the boys spotted our bandages and quickly asked, "What in the heck happened?" We both sputtered through the highlights, and then Phil asked, "Were you at least wearing a life jacket?" Simultaneously I said "yes" and Sheila said "no." We were busted, and Phil was thoroughly disgusted. That was the beginning of a lifetime of laughable and memorable near misses.

Pushing Buttons

Shortly after we married, a fear overwhelmed me that turned my emotions into hamburger meat, a fear that I had made a tragic mistake and wasn't capable of making this work. I really didn't know myself and didn't know how to be a wife. I had no mentoring for a good marriage. I didn't know how to let Phil be a husband and the leader of our home. Any authority he imposed I filtered through the iron hand that ruled my childhood home by Carl. He too, had no healthy family model to follow, as his childhood was littered with arguing and abuse. Late one night we pulled into the apartment complex parking lot. I can't really remember what buttons I pushed, I just knew how to push past his limits and send Phil into a tirade. Deep down, I thought surely he'll leave me sooner or later, and I preferred sooner because I was scared of myself. In his frustration, he hit me. Not hard, not intentionally, he actually took my hand and hit the steering wheel. It didn't matter; I had pushed him to the edge. I wanted to see if he could get to this point, and he did. He failed my test. That was it. I was ready to run. He hit me. The circumstances surrounding the outburst didn't matter, it didn't even matter that it was entirely my fault. All that mattered was that I could provoke him to this point. It was his final exam, and he failed.

The apologies poured out of his mouth, but I couldn't hear them. We went inside, and I was a zombie. He went to bed, and I lay on the couch. I took the keys to the car, and I left. I drove around for hours, trying so hard to make sense of it all. I wanted to run like I had wanted to run my entire childhood. I was determined to get a divorce and end it before it got too complicated. I was flogging myself, setting myself up for failure, hearing the words of Carl that were engraved in my head, "You are a good-for-nothing whore. You don't have sense to get out of a shower of s--t. You are as sorry as they come. You are so *g-d* stupid, you smell." Those words were implanted in my head since I was a little girl: those words lived in my consciousness. They swirled in and out of my thoughts like March winds. When I heard them, I perceived Phil as Carl. I was loving him through my filter of abuse. There was always a wall around my heart. I couldn't feel his love; I could only feel Carl's abuse. I knew Phil wanted desperately to break through that wall.

I heard a voice tell me, "You've got to go back. You can't run. If you leave, you'll never go back." I couldn't leave a love we both fought so hard to find. I returned. I forgave.

We started over. I set boundaries: "You can never hit me again. You don't have a second chance. You can never hit me again, no matter how mad you get." It was a turning point in our relationship. I had reason to stay, to forgive, and he had reason to change. That was neither the first nor the last explosive outburst, but he never hit me again. I spent years trying to push him away, trying to prove my point: that he would leave. I know he told me he would never leave me and always love me, but his words were meaningless until they stood the test of time and the test of my antagonism.

I had a lot of growing to do, a lot of healing to do, a lot of forgiving to do, and a long way to go to get through the layers of pain that tainted my every thought and controlled my every move. Sadly, we were both mad at God for our sad childhoods; we were running from God, running from our pain. At least, we had each other to run to.

CHAPTER 17

Death of the Secret

My group of rafters has survived the last rapid, and the raft is pulled by a motor boat through the beautiful surreal lake for the remainder of the trip. The warm sunshine bakes my chilled body dry. We lay back and soak in the tranquility of the sound of the birds, of the wind, and the calm of the river. Alone now for almost twenty-four hours with no bad memories, no panic attacks and no anxious feelings. My mind is finally at rest. It is not cluttered with a million details. Rest is peaceful. I feel the adrenalin rushing and have that wonderful sense of feeling alive. This ride down the river has been a rite of passage that will forever mark my life as a time of cleansing and a day of forgiveness; the day I finally forgive myself and all those people in my life who hurt me.

Even though I'll always cherish these moments alone, I am so thankful I'm not alone in this world, so thankful I let my walls down. I let love into my life. I have so many wonderful people in my life, and I am so grateful for their love and encouragement. The silence is broken, the lies revealed, flooded like the river. I will share my pain and now my gain. I breathe in the crisp air floating down the Chattooga River and hear the song of the river. What an awesome sound, the sound of forgiveness.

I'm ready to let go of the ring. I pull it out of my pocket once again. I'm ready to throw it in the river. I have held on to the ring and all that it represents for much too long. I hold it in my hand and feel the rough stones and the piercing prongs that hold the sapphires in place. Why now am I so drawn to the sapphire ring, the ring that I dug out of my old, red, furry Christmas stocking so many years ago? I still have that stocking, now old and tattered with a retro plastic face of Santa and nappy, white, fur top with red-fur footing. That Christmas morning I admired the beauty of the ring: eight sapphires sparkling among eight diamonds. As pretty as the ring is, it made me sick to accept it from him. I liked the ring, but detested what it stood for…the purchase of my continued silence. In all the years of marriage to my Mother, he never gave her a gift ring.

The sun catches the diamonds and the sapphires. The sparkle draws attention from my comrade cliff-jumpers. "What a pretty ring. Why are you holding it over the water?"

"I … I don't know." I search for words to even begin to tell them, as the tears stream down my face.

By June 16, 1987, Phil and I had been married nearly two years. We were visiting my sisters in Mobile and trying desperately to stay involved in their lives. In the middle of the night, we were all awakened from a deep sleep by a loud banging at the front door. It was the leaded glass pane front door to 465 Briar Patch Place, and someone was banging on the glass so hard the door was vibrating like it would break into a million pieces. It was around 2 a.m., and it was so hard to understand what was going on as we stumbled to consciousness. It was all a blur, as if it were happening in a smoky fog of slow motion.

There stood a uniformed police officer who asked, "Is this the home of James Carl Rivers?" Mother immediately started screaming to the top of her lungs, "What is it, what is it, what is it? Oh my God, Oh my God, Oh my God, Oh God! No, NO! Oh God!" I peered over my Mother's shoulder as the police officer continued, "Please calm down, Miss. There was an automobile accident about 10 p.m., and Mr. Rivers was killed."

Through my Mother's screaming, the officer proceeded to tell us how Carl's car was struck by a train at a rail crossing. He was pronounced dead on the scene, and his body had been taken to the morgue.

He handed us a small white piece of paper with the phone number to the morgue where his body had been taken, while Mother continued screaming at the top of her lungs. She ran into the middle of the street and lay down on the pavement. Her blood curling screams could be heard for miles.

The day Carl died is etched in my memory forever, a still picture of the events of that day, June 16, 1987. It had been a smoldering hot summer day, and we had gone to the beach and to the "Night in Old Mobile" festival. It had been three years since I ran away from home, but I struggled to return to 465 Briar Patch Place, continuing my pilgrimage to keep an open door to my sisters. During those years, my Mother had sunk into a dark depression. With the fear of "the secret" buried again, Carl had been free to return to the pattern of severe abuse, beating her into the ground daily. He was on his best behavior for about a year after I left home, and allowed her to stay home and not teach school. After the shock of my disclosure wore off, he went back to his abusive controlling behavior.

Carl had worked the night shift that night, so I knew we wouldn't see much of him. My goal was to check on my sisters and make sure they were okay. I wanted to make sure the evil of sexual abuse had not bled into their lives, though they suffered plenty from the turmoil in the home. Carl came home from work and slept for a couple of hours. It was around 9 a.m., and he got up, spoke to Phil and me coldly, and headed out the door. My Mother followed him out, and we could hear them yelling in the driveway. Mother wanted him to spend the day with us. We obviously wanted him gone. He drove off, and she followed him down Fontaine Drive, running after the car.

He pulled over, got out of his car, came around to the back and screamed at her, "If you g-d ever follow me again, I will kill you where you stand, do you g-d f-----g hear me!" She yelled back, "God won't let you continue to treat me this way!"

He got back in the car and sped away. He was going to the farm about a hundred miles north near my grandparents to work with his cows, and he had to be back to the plastics plant in Mobile for the eleven o'clock shift. She returned home minutes later, shaking and crying. She wouldn't go with us that day, and I'm sure she stayed and wallowed in her pity. She told me that she had recently opened a checking account in her name, and she was trying to make plans to leave. Apparently, she awoke when he said, "I will kill you." Those turned out to be the last words he spoke to her.

Now, with him dead, we all began grappling with a new reality. Phil had to go to the morgue to identify Carl, but it wasn't until the *Mobile News* was delivered the next morning, that I finally believed it to be true. It was on the front page. A photo of the mangled car and the headline read, "Man Killed in Train Wreck." Could it be that this tyrant was out of my life for good? It was as if the gates of freedom had been flung wide open.

My Mother sat and laughed, all morning long she laughed. People were dropping off food, and she laughed. She was trying to make funeral arrangements, and she laughed. Her breakdown was a blink away.

Chaos reigned. There was a funeral to arrange and attend. To find a redeeming quality to speak over Carl's casket was our task. Our duty was to give him a respectful service, and I went along with the charade, even though I wanted to cremate him and throw his ashes in the trash. It was my Mother's obligation to convince everyone that he was now in heaven. It was a difficult mission to convince even herself, much less anyone who knew him. She clung to one passage that she distorted to help her believe Carl would be in Heaven. It was the Gospel account of the thief on the cross, dying but calling to Jesus to go with Him. I know Carl did not live his life as a believer, but she clung to the hope that, if the thief dying on the cross could be saved at the last instant, even Carl would be saved or could have asked for salvation as he lay dying.

Miracles happen, and I certainly don't have all the answers. I think it was Billy Graham who said the dying thief's salvation account is the only instance of a deathbed confession in the Bible, given once "that no man should despair and only once that no man should presume." I believe if Carl did indeed call upon the name of Jesus in that wrecked car, in his mangled state, he would be forgiven. That is the awesome God we serve, and that is God's plan of salvation that Jesus' blood on the cross took the wrath for our sin. He may not hear the words "well done good and faithful servant," but he would be spared from hell.

More important than to question Carl's salvation, this was an opportunity to search my own heart. It terrified me to think that one day someone would stand over my casket and speak of my life. I wanted no question mark, no doubt of my salvation and my relationship with Jesus. I prayed that God would begin to show me the things in my life that didn't please Him. When you pray, God answers. Over the next ten years, God began to show me all the sin in my life, and I am still in a season of conviction and repentance. God is sovereign.

We managed to tell the preacher that Carl was a hard worker, a devoted family man, and that he loved nature, as he raised cows. That encompassed the entire service. The preacher, having never met him, knew he had to stretch, so stretch he did, and it was still a brief funeral service. I did not know how to express my emotions. None of us did. I cried, but it was out of relief. I was so relieved that the fear was gone. When he lived, I was so afraid. I trembled in his presence. I anticipated his tirades, and I lived in fear of what he could do to me and others, not only my Mother and sisters but other young children who crossed his path. I clung tight to Phil, and he walked the four of us through the entire ordeal. In those moments, he became the patriarch of the family. In a disturbed way, I thought I caused Carl's death. I thought the powers-that-be listened, as I begged for his demise. I wanted to kill him a million times, and now his life had ended in a gruesome way. It was justice to me. We walked through his death, confused over life. There was not much to honor in his life and a lot to reclaim in our own lives.

My Mother was so helpless. I had to lead the family through the mess, as always. Mother was able to do very little; she seemed unable to function. In a few short weeks after his death, she felt the freedom to acknowledge that my accusations *"could be"* true. She needed me and realized fast that, only a few short years before, she had turned her back on me. Now that the danger was gone, and he was dead, it would have been even easier for me to walk away. I wished many times I could have walked away, but I accepted my responsibility, and Phil remained the saint, as we had to immerse ourselves in every crisis, the main one being an unstable mother. As usual, roles reversed, and I had to care for her.

She spent money in outlandish ways, as if it grew on trees and she had a forest-full. She sold the cattle, cashed out the insurance policies. She blew through the money buying things, a pool for the back yard, a Cadillac, a home addition, a pool table. There was no thought for taking care of the future, for saving, for the responsibility of providing for my sisters. The only thought was the immediate gratification through spending money. Then the bottom fell out. She lost her job. Fortunately, God provided, even in her darkest days.

The Secret Lingers

To this day, I examine my soul. I ponder the secret and its power. I don't know how I kept the secret for so many years; it was a merry-go-round with no beginning and no end. I don't know how I plastered a smile on my face and fooled the world. I dug deep in my soul and found resources to survive in the most horrendous of circumstances. I try so hard to figure out the mystery. I felt like I had kept quiet and silently endured the abuse for my Mother. I felt like I did it to hide the shame. I felt like I did it, because I didn't want anyone to ever know. He drilled fear deep inside me. I wasn't strong enough to open my mouth. I wasn't smart enough to find the words to communicate what was happening behind closed doors. I was so young when he took control of my mind and my emotions. Like most children, I didn't know the words to even begin to describe what he was doing to me. The secret branded by soul. I knew from instinct and from my feelings that it was horrible. At my core, I felt depleted of all self-worth and full of fear. It was easier to keep the secret than to reveal it. It was easier to walk in silence than to risk everything.

He groomed me for years, and in that grooming, he convinced me that speaking would mean death and destruction. Death and destruction for me and for those I loved. I feared destroying my Mother, our home and any chance I had to survive. If I threatened telling, I suffered great consequences. I suffered, but my Mother suffered more. I couldn't take it. I couldn't stand to see her abused. It hurt worse than my own abuse. It became easier to seal my lips and comply. I kept praying for change. I clung to a day of deliverance, not knowing when it would come or how, but I clung to my faith that deliverance would come. I clung to a dream of peace and serenity, of safety and solace.

Life unfolds, and the secret still plagues me, as I'm sure the secret of sexual abuse plagues millions. Up to this point in time, I had never felt delivered from the secret I kept. The secret gives the perpetrator the power and gives the victim the burden. The secret destroys a life from the inside out. It festers, and without a voice, it shackles emotional health and freedom. Maybe it was a mistake, perhaps the biggest mistake of my life, but I could *never* tell, and there are millions of others out there just like me who could never tell. There are millions who have *never* told.

Brick Walls

Phil and I put down roots. We moved to our second home and had a precious daughter and son. In the early '90s, I was trying to be a good mother, a good wife, a good Realtor, and a good person, still trying hard to peel away the wax coating of shame. I wanted my children to look perfect and my home to be perfect, clean, and cozy. I worked to conjure up the latest recipe. A true Martha Stewart I attempted to be. I was trying so hard to impress, instead of trying so hard to bless. The outside looked perfect, but the inside was a mess, and I was treading water to stay sane. We, as women are the thermostat in the home; we control comfort. I so desperately wanted to create magical moments for my family, wonderful memories for my children. I wanted to give them all the

215

encouragement and all the nurturing I so lacked in my own childhood. I struggled to stay sane for them. They deserved the kind of childhood I had longed for.

The trauma I lived with for years became more and more real. The buried memories began to surface. I could not cope. I would see Carl, alive in my house during the day. I ran from him, and I ran from the memories, but he was in my waking thoughts, and he was in my nightmares. The depression and anxiety became more than I could bear. I spiraled down into a dark hole. It was a time in my life when I absolutely had it all, and I had no reason to feel so desperate. The crescendo of despair had been building since that night of my suicide attempt. I internalized the self-hatred and the pain. There were so many unresolved issues in my life and so many things I had to accept as they were, with no justification, no answers, and no accountability from anyone. I could not scrub the abuse from my memory. I could not claw the shame from my face. In my early twenties, I worked so darned hard and kept so darned busy that I had no time to pity myself or to focus on the past. But now, things were different.

I was on a tight rope between sanity and insanity. I hallucinated, seeing Carl vividly in my closet. I woke up that morning and took care of my children. I was quietly polishing the routines of my life, the routine of breakfast, dressing, diaper changes, laundry, dishes, Sesame Street, Barney, more diaper changes, snacks, and round again. In my routine, I had time to ponder. I fought the memories but I was delirious. They were attacking, and as I worked, I would try so hard not to think about them, but I became obsessed with them – I had Pink Elephant syndrome. I never saw him in the casket. I thought, "What if that wasn't really him? What if he didn't die that night and it was someone else and it was all a plot for him to go somewhere else and start over." Crazy thoughts! I opened my bedroom closet, and there he was with that evil grin. I fell to my knees and covered my eyes. When I finally removed my hands, he, of course, wasn't there, but my heart was beating out of my torso.

I experienced bouts of anxiety so severe I couldn't breathe, as if an elephant were sitting on my chest. I would smell the sulfur from the plastics plant, the smell that always engulfed Carl. I would hyperventilate and try to conceal my suffering. I tried squelching the toxic inner voices; I tried to find that inner voice that kept me living on faith and will. There was a battle raging inside, a battle that I fought alone.

Phil would reach for me at night, but my mind was absent, lost in turmoil, and I did not want to be touched. To this day, if I get so engrossed in memories of the past, even a kiss can feel wrong, suffocating me. I suffered in silence many nights. Phil was so sensitive to whatever vibes I released, and he would constantly ask the question, "What is wrong with you, why are you so distant?" I never wanted to hurt him. I never wanted him to know the torment, or how after all these years of marriage, I still suffered in silence. Some nights, he knew I was fighting some vague demons, and he would relate it to his abuse and neglect as a boy. His home was littered with beer cans from his mother's consumption and his father's frustration beyond forgiveness.

Phil, like most men, wanted to fix it. He wanted to fix me. He wanted me to choose to forget it all and never relive a moment of the pain. He offered an analogy: "It was unfortunate, it was a bad situation. But like being stopped at a traffic light, when the light changes you *go*. You move past it, and you choose to not let it affect you. You choose to not look back." I so wish it was that easy. I can't explain it, but those feelings of the sexual, physical, and emotional abuse, those memories of times when I was so vulnerable and so demoralized can bleed like a crusty scab scratched open.

Sometimes, Phil would touch me, and I would feel Carl's hands. He would hold me, and I would smell Carl's stale breath. Some nights, intimacy with Phil was a struggle, and Phil would think it was his problem. No, it was my problem. When you can't find the mental strength to make love to your husband, whom you love beyond words, it compounds your feelings of inadequacy even more. I became very accomplished at controlling my body during sex with my stepfather, and I struggled to relax during intimacy years later. The anxiety escalated, and as they say, the more I tried not to think about pink elephants, the more I thought about pink elephants. I wanted Phil to be happy, I wanted to hold my marriage together, and sex is an important part of marriage. I wanted to make passionate love to my husband without Carl's ghost in the room. Every 24 hours, this conflict of past memory and present desire made me dread the night.

I would try to sleep but would dream the same nightmares that had plagued me for years. I could not get the lid back on "Pandora's box." The box of vileness had opened, and I couldn't stuff all the junk back in fast enough. I wasn't equipped to deal with the memories, to feel the anguish and the sting that surrounded the abuse. I dreamed he was on top of me, and I couldn't pry him off. I dreamed everyone in my life was circled around me, while he was on top of me. I had dreams of driving over a bridge, and the water from the bridge would be rising faster than I could get across, and I would wake up drowning in the car. I would dream Carl was in my bed, and I couldn't push him out, even though his body had decomposed. His skin would be peeling off in my hands as I clawed at his face. My rage frightened me. I came unglued.

There were nights in my dreams that the little girl with long black hair, cropped bangs, all dressed up with frilly ankle socks and red velvet dress would be running through a maze trying to open doors that were all locked. Carl would be running behind her, beating her with a belt, and he would keep beating and beating until blood would pour. Others couldn't see the blood because the dress was red. My Mother would be on the other side of a glass wall, and I could see her, but I couldn't get to her. I couldn't find a way around the wall.

The shame in my life festered into a self-hatred so severe that inside, I believed I did nothing right. Internal torture repeated damaging dialogue, day in and day out. I flogged myself with those thoughts, those feelings. I still fight them. I gain strength by speaking God's truth out loud. When my mind is idle, the words are louder, and when my mind is busy, I can push them into a small cranny diminishing their strength. I feel the spiritual warfare, and I fight the battle; the victory is my sanity.

Night after night, I dreamed of the state of terror I'd experienced. Some nights I didn't even want to go to sleep. I would lie in bed squeezing my pillow in anguish. My pillow would be soaked with tears as Phil snored. I buried my face to soak up the tears, and I sank deeper and deeper into my silent suffering. I tried so hard to numb my pain. I used drugs and alcohol to try to forget. I felt I couldn't let anyone know I was coming apart at the seams, especially Phil, because our life together was at stake. The children needed me, and he needed me. Driven and panicked, I struggled to keep it together. Though I wanted to crawl out of my skin, I had to keep my smile plastered in place; I had to be sane for them in the midst of my meltdown.

As much as I thought I was keeping my breakdown under wraps, Phil knew I needed help beyond what he could personally provide. We agreed that he would contact Charter Peachford Hospital to learn what treatment options were available. He suggested admitting me, and I begged and pleaded for another way. I couldn't fathom my children having memories of me being in a mental institution, and I certainly couldn't bear the thought of Phil reliving the agonizing memories of visiting his own mother in the state mental hospital. I had fought so hard for my sanity, for my own family, stability, for happiness, and I was not about to give up now.

Getting Help

To begin, we settled on intensive therapy three days a week. After my first visit, I was put on medications – about every flavor possible. I had been diagnosed with a chemical imbalance and Post Traumatic Stress Syndrome, and the therapy and medications were working to fix me. The medication helped, but it numbed me. I couldn't feel the anxiety, but I also couldn't feel joy. I simply couldn't and didn't feel. Anti-depressants were not my drugs of choice, and though they helped for a season, they did not solve my problems.

On the other hand, the therapy took me to a place of understanding. I began to truly believe that I was not to blame for what happened. Therapy gave me the right to say that I did not have the power to prevent the abuse. I faced the reality that it really was *so awful*. It was years of ruthless torment. My Mother had always dismissed my pain, never acknowledging the years of anguish I had suffered. Therapy also gave me license to be mad, to be angry and to channel that anger into good. I went on a journey to relive parts of my childhood that had been robbed. The therapist asked, "What in your childhood can you fix? What childhood dreams can you still pursue?"

I loved to color, so I took an oil painting class. I'll never forget the first words of my art instructor, "I'm not going to teach you how to paint, but I'm going to teach you how to *see*." I needed to see the beauty I missed in my childhood. I needed to find the beauty within. I also chased the dream of acting and even landed a lame part on a TV commercial. I spent this season of therapy attempting to discover more of myself. I spent a spell just enjoying time alone with myself and slowing down to a more reasonable pace. I began to get more help in the house and with the kids. I learned that life can be good without having it all together all of the time. One of my favorite sayings is, "We may not have it together, but together we have it all." I could do enough, be enough, and have enough to be content. I decided that was what God wanted for me – contentment in the day without worry for tomorrow. As Rick Warren writes in *The Purpose-Driven Life*, "We are human beings, not human doings."

I stopped entertaining every single weekend trying to earn the neighborhood popularity contest. I started in the early '90s attending a Women's Christian Retreat about "balance in life." It was held at Calloway Gardens, a beautiful natural park setting to rest and refresh in God's presence. My soul found quiet there, and I was able to open up to God and His will for my life. During these pilgrimages, I grew in my relationship with Christ, as I deepened my faith and my emotional strength. I began to fall in love with Jesus. I began to trust Him with my life. I began to receive His love, His grace and His mercy. I began to understand His sovereignty. In turn, my Lord began to lance the bitterness in my soul. My annual sabbatical there has given me the power to write this book and expose my vulnerabilities.

Phil and I also began taking special time together and, slowly, through the years, I have walked out of my darkness into the light of Christ. Slowly the memories became bearable, even to the degree that I am able to not only share with a therapist, but with others. It was as if bright light began shining in my dark places, and the terrible creatures and memories scurried from the light, or were at least too blinded to attack me. I believe that light came from God; He heard my pleas for help and brought the light of His life and word into my battles with darkness.

CHAPTER 18

Healing Discoveries

My river adventure has helped me find peace. Absorbed in God's creation, I now know Him in the beauty of today; there is so much that life has to offer and to appreciate. An attitude of gratitude is a great place for healing to start. The harsh memories of yesterday seem light years away when we spend time alone with Him and in Him.

Yet being a solitary traveler will be a challenge today, as I never like to be alone, but I know it is the best medicine for now. I miss my family at this moment, and I can't wait to return home and hold them. I need my home, and I need the love my sweet family showers upon me. I could never be a gypsy. However, I know this alone time is both good and important for me. Finally, a peace, that I have waited years to enjoy, has come over me, and it feels wonderful. I can't wait to share this miracle with them. I am a survivor. I overcame abuse as surely as I defeated the Chattooga River.

What an incredible rush I experienced today, and so fitting that I chose a brush with death to let it all go. I washed my past off of me today on the river, never, ever to be tortured by it again. I finally accepted that I wasn't the bad person; it was Carl who was bad. All those ugly things he spoke over me and into me, that tragically I believed for so long, are not truth. God has delivered me from the valley of the shadow of death and I will fear no evil. Carl was evil, and he is gone. I trust that Carl is in God's hands.

Today was a day of great fun battling nature, with its power and force, and battling myself, and I have gained a true respect for both. I look back at the Chattooga River and bid farewell, with a promise to return. I thank God for this experience and I pray I can take these treasured moments with me and hold them close to my soul forever. I feel happy, truly happy with myself and with my life, knowing there will be more challenges to come. Now I will go home and try to live every moment being the best person I can be, forever changed by this river and by this time. It is evidence of God's glory to visit the edge and return victorious and to survive in every challenge life deals us. I am ready now to accept my past so I can move on to my future.

Surrender as Advanced Therapy

My journey has been a long and winding road, and one that I've walked through by faith and faith alone. Jesus raised Lazarus from the dead, and Jesus healed me from the abuse. I believe Jesus to be my Savior, and I believe in His healing and resurrection power. I believe He saves and He heals, and I believe that He has been with me since the first vile touch and through the burn of abuse that seared my soul. I know I did not deserve such treatment, but as Romans 8:28 says, "All things work together for good for those who love Him, and are called according to His purpose."

If the good is to speak through this book to women and men in this world who are struggling with child sexual abuse issues, abandonment or fatherless issues, self-hatred, self-destructive or confidence issues, if sharing my struggle is my calling, then I embrace it as my purpose. I don't question the calling. Who am I to question a sovereign God who calls the waves back to shore time and time again? I may never understand why this happened to me. I didn't ask for this; neither did I want to turn myself inside out to share my experience. I did however hear God's voice telling me to write my story so it touches a life that needs a touch. This is my assignment. How do I know? I've felt since I was a little girl that I had a purpose in this world. I felt that I was different and, in a very comforting way, that God's hand was on me.

The fear has never left me, yet as an adult, I've never felt totally abandoned in it. I have some fear of what the words on these pages will do to my life now, but I have greater power drawing me to finish this task, above all else. I have to remember God that has His ways, and He will take me through the fear to the other side. He will lead, and I will follow.

Even at the lowest point of my life, even when I was at the end of my rope on suicide's door, I felt that if God had taken me that night, He would not have deserted me; He would have been right there with me. I now know beyond any doubt that God's grace won't take you beyond His mercy. I know He was there, and I know absolutely He opened that car door when I was intoxicated with sleeping pills and alcohol.

I have known the kind of fear that only another kindred spirit knows who has suffered at the hands of an abuser. I wish I could describe it more vividly. It is unimaginable and unexplainable unless actually experienced. It starts in the pit of the stomach and rises to the top of the head, choking every bit of happiness from your life. Many call it anxiety, and with anxiety, frequently comes depression. I have battled depression and I have battled anxiety, and I know the difference. Many doctors say that chemical imbalances in the brain promote depression. I cope with this often when I can't seem to stop myself from spiraling down into the blackness of the hole that is always there waiting for me, and once there, it is so difficult to climb out. It's a spiral down into darkness where I become isolated in the pain.

When I am in that place, I don't want to talk about it, and I don't want to bring anyone else into it. I want to suffer alone. When I let myself go to that place of total brokenness, I cry agonizing tears, and my heart aches. The ache doesn't leave after the tears are dried. I've screamed in anxiety to God, "I am so tired of hurting! Please God, please, I beg you to take this cup." I know how the bottom feels and am searching for the top, clutching the rope to pull myself up.

I cringe to admit it, but I hated God for a time. I blamed and feared God, and I really did not know how to reach out for Him. I held a distorted view of God with two failed father figures on earth. I was in search of myself without God, a self I could never find. I sought to fill a bottomless pit with anything and everything but Him, and none of it brought me joy. I know God is all-knowing and all-powerful, and for this reason, I resented Him for my fate. If God loved me, why did I suffer so? Why do I struggle so emotionally? If only for the purpose of this calling? I've learned not to ask why. Why death? Why war? Why disease? God knows and I can trust Him.

Over time, I have decided that the good and the bad we experience can be for God's glory. The words that have poured out of my heart have continued to cleanse my soul. It has been a journey through the past, bringing new perspective and new growth for the present, and maturity for the future. I understand now how to keep myself in a state of joy and optimism. I have learned to put the painful memories in a place of insignificance. They don't define me.

Reaching Out

In my darkest days, God started to lay the groundwork for this book. He knew my purpose. I feel there is a purpose to my pain, one so much greater than I could comprehend and a purpose I still don't completely understand. This is who I am, and no matter how much I've tried, or how much my Mother wishes to sweep this tragic story under the rug, it happened, and I have to live with it inside of me. Only God enables me to bear it. God has proven Himself to me time and time again. God has given me so many miracles, from saving my life the night I attempted to end it, sending my true love, giving me my precious children, to meeting me on the Chattooga River where I totally surrendered my pain and my life to His mercy. That was truly a glorious mountaintop experience, top to bottom.

God's plan of free will gave Carl the choice to be vile and evil. It was Carl perpetrating the cruelty, not God. It was not God's will that this evil occurred, but Carl's choice to sin. I truly believe that Carl was under the influence of satanic forces.

God has taught me so much about how to walk through my pain. God has always been so close, even when I felt that He was so far. He showed me that neither Phil, nor my children, nor my friends, nor drugs, nor alcohol, nor my Mother's love – that absolutely nothing, could fill the hole in my heart but *Him*. I collapsed into the arms of Christ. As God's Word says in Isaiah 40:31, "Those who wait for the Lord will gain new strength. They will mount up with wings like eagles, they will run and not get tired, they will walk and not become weary."

I am determined to stand strong in my faith and in God's Word. It is a journey that pulls me close to His side. I can't walk ahead; I can't walk behind; I can't walk away; I must walk beside Him. I have to open His Word, the Bible, and believe what His Word tells me, "There is no condemnation for those who are in Christ Jesus," (Romans 8:1) and that "I can do all things through Christ who strengthens me." (Philippians 4:13) I must let His Word wash over me, comfort me, cleanse me, teach me, heal me.

It is my journey and my mission to share my walk with the many hurting people who find it so hard to love themselves past the abuse. I was sacrificed to perversion, but that does not make me perverted. Filth covered me, but that does not make me dirty. I look at God's love as a washcloth that has washed me inside out. I may never erase the abuse and its results from my memory bank, but I can stand firm in my faith, I can diminish their significance, and reclaim my life and my clear mind.

I know God has a plan for my life, but unfortunately, Satan also has a plan. I have a choice, and I choose God's plan.

CHAPTER 19

Beams of Blessings

Though the river is soothing, the sands in the hourglass keep falling slowly. I am roaming through the rooms in my mind. Doors of each of these rooms have been closed for a long season. I run so hard day and night to keep control of my world, just as I did as a child. I flee the memories, racing faster and faster, until this year they caught up with me.

Being an over-achiever is not always a blessing, and for me, it's a curse. I truly think I can be a happier person if I can only force myself to slow down and take that mound of pressure for perfection off my shoulders. I never give myself a break. I am so hard on myself. There's a voice that continues to beat me up inside, the same voice that beat me as a child. I am just beginning, after these six months or so of therapy, to understand and to dissect the destructive programming of my childhood. I have to harness my drive to allow time to simply enjoy life and my family.

I can accept the pain in my past, just as I can embrace this wonderful life I have today. I have to channel this energy into productive means. I can't change a thing in my past, and I can't change what people did or didn't do, but I can commit the very best of me to Phil and to my children. I desperately want to live my life in peace and joy.

I ride along listening to the music and allowing God to put His branding on my heart: The song and the words hold so much depth and meaning. I know God's spirit helped write these treasured words:

> From the mountains to the valleys,
> From the rivers to the sea.

Every hand that reaches out.
Every hand that reaches out to offer peace.
Every simple act of mercy.
Every step to kingdom come.
All the hope in every hope in every heart
Will speak what love has done.
For as long as I shall live I will testify to love.
I'll be the witness in the silences when words
are not enough.
With every breath that I take I will give thanks
to God above.
For as long as I shall live I will testify.
I will testify to love. [7]

I miss my babies, Ashley and Jacob. I can't wait to hold their faces in my hands and feel their arms around my neck. Their tender voices echo in my head, "I want to hold you," Ashley says. "Mommy, watch me," my four-year-old Jacob will repeat.

I feel compelled to do a better job than my Mother. I want to protect my babies from the evil of this world. I want to spare them pain, and if I can't, I want to at least be there with open arms to ease their grief. I want to be the mother I never had. I don't want to fail; I can't fail at this most important job. There is too much at risk. Two lives depend on Phil and me to give them what they need to develop healthy emotional lives. I want to shatter the cycle of abuse. They look to me to recognize the harmful traits that are embedded in me and to make a conscious decision to change. To destroy the cycle of abuse takes a conscious decision; it takes a dedicated commitment. Parenting skills come from what is learned, but when those skills are caustic and cursed, they must be abandoned and replaced with skills that seek to nurture and empower. I know I face an enormous responsibility, an enormous challenge.

I had to learn coping techniques that kept me from lashing out at my first child, Ashley. I would feel the rage boil up in me, and I would pull my hand back when she frustrated me beyond normal control. As my hand was swinging forward, I caught myself. I stopped it in mid-air. I fell to my knees and began to pray, "Dear God, please don't let me lash out at my children in uncontrolled rage. Please don't let me leave scars on their hearts and minds that will never be erased. Please help me discipline with control."

I never hit her, I never grabbed her, and I never shook her, though many times I wanted to. It wasn't because of anything she did or didn't do as a little child; it was because there was so much anger and rage inside of me that had no place to go. The rage from my childhood boiled inside me and could have boiled into destruction. I have taken so many punches in my life; it was as if they were still inside me, lurking to jab at someone else. I see how the cycle of abuse perpetuates itself. I was determined to NOT be a statistic. I was determined to break my generational sins. I was determined to change future generations from this child forward.

I started to make a list of what I wanted and needed so desperately as a child yet never received, and tried to meet those needs in my children. I needed a tender touch, an innocent tender touch. I would softly rub my fingers over their forehead from the time they were infants. It soothed them. I needed hugs and kisses. I showered them with hugs and kisses daily. I needed someone to look into my eyes and listen to my words. I tried to bow down on my knees to hear their sweet words, to give them the time and attention to express themselves. I needed healthy boundaries without contradictions. I tried to teach them truth and honesty and respect and tried even harder to mentor those values. I needed to hear the words "I love you." There isn't a day that goes by that we don't say, "I love you," not a single day those words don't bounce off the walls in our home. Children need to be seen, they need to be heard, they need to be believed and they need to be loved. If these were in every family's constitution, perhaps we could eliminate child sexual abuse forever.

I implemented a consistent pattern of discipline for both children that has proven to be quite successful. The "three strikes rule" has worked remarkably well, and consistency has been the key. Strike one for unacceptable behavior is a warning, followed by a count to three for the behavior to change. Strike two for the same offense is a count of three for the behavior to change, followed by a trip to time out (usually a minute per year of age). And strike three is a spanking. I never gave them a spanking in anger. I always counted to ten backward before I laid a hand on them. During my countdown, calm would surround me, and I would punish them with respect and love. Neither of my children had more spankings than can be counted on one hand, and all of those were for either lying or outright acts of disrespect.

I have been consistent since they were toddlers, even to the point where they have, at times, put themselves in time-out after committing an offense. I can't take all the credit, because they have been model children, and they have had a wonderful role model for a father. Phil has supported this policy and practiced it himself. He's never disciplined them without thorough explanation of unacceptable behavior and consequences.

As a victim and survivor of abuse, I had feared the same fate for my children. I taught my children since the time they could speak that no one ever touches their private parts. Private parts were always defined in our home as those parts covered by a swimsuit. I taught them how to say "NO" loudly. I told them to come and tell me immediately. I carried the fear for years that someone would violate my children. I have remained acutely aware of their safety and protective of their lives. I pray that their innocence is preserved. That is the responsibility of every mother, to protect her children.

'Happy Family'

A blessing is a supernatural favor from God, and my greatest blessing is the family God has given me. I could have never achieved this in my own strength. By my own effort alone, I could never have been the wife or mother I wanted to be in order to foster health and happiness in my home. The greatest success in my life is my family, to which I give God the glory. The most joy I squeeze from life is my family. I don't take a moment of this joy for granted. I revel in these moments. I defeated the odds, and if I can beat the odds, anyone can. God does not show preference of persons, what He does for one He'll do for you.

Where there is a will, there is a way. There is a "D Day" in everyone's life, a fork in the road that leads to either a path of destruction or a path of happiness. I thank God that he kept nudging me down the right road. I thank God I can say "goodbye" to my old friend Fear for a while and taste the sweet joy of life.

I believe God's Word when He says, "Ask and it will be given to you; seek and you will find; knock and the door will be opened to you. For everyone who asks receives; he who seeks finds; and to him who knocks, the door will be opened."(Matthew 7:7-8)

Several years have now passed since my adventurous river rafting retreat and I have continued to journal sporadically, especially during times that move me.

Journal Entry April 2001

I squeeze the sand between my toes, hearing the irresistible sound of the crashing ocean waves. I long to keep this peace in my heart always. I gaze into my life as I hear the waves kiss the shore. I am so blessed to have discovered peace in my life. Maybe not 24/7, but I'll take these moments. I love the beach, the sounds and smells, all of which bring back days of running wild with my sand bucket and my inflatable duck around my waist. As I enjoy the ocean breeze and soak in the sun, I watch Jacob digging his hole to Neverland in the sand. With sweet patience, he digs deeper and deeper, gazing up at me with that gentle smile of a little boy soon to be knocking on adolescence's door. He shares my passion for the beach, a place of safe haven to truly relax. The ocean is my sacred place where the agenda is only to sit still, reflect and refresh. Oh, how I have missed writing! Why have I not picked up a pen to journal in so many years? This is my passion.

My young lady, Ashley, has become a woman, a charming young woman. Overnight she has blossomed into this exceptional human being with a heart of gold and an anointed spirit that embraces goodness. She too adores the ocean and all it does to refresh the soul. For all I've done wrong as a mother, I praise God that I did some things right because my two children are two of the most amazing people I know. They love so unconditionally and exhibit such respect for others and a refreshing sense of responsibility for their age.

We are in such a busy season in our lives, that I pray we take the time to keep our bonds and connections with our children strong. We are spending the week with them on Amelia Island before school starts. Phil is stuck in the beach house making calls for the new company that he is getting off the ground. I'm enjoying the day waiting for my cell phone to start going off with real estate calls. It has been slow for a Monday, but I realized I probably can't get a signal on the beach, and the calls are going to voice mail. "Yes!"

What a Kodak Moment, and, of course, I don't have my camera. Jacob is digging away with determination. He exclaimed, "My hole has been taken over by a swarm of minnows!" The waves are etching closer to my chair, but I hate to lay my pen down. There is so much I want to write about.

It is a special time for insight and reflection that rarely comes my way.

But the pleas for "Mommy" are persistent and I lay down my pen and enjoyed a leisurely walk down the beach hand-in-hand with my son. I listen to his bigger-than-life questions and assumptions. I shut off everything in this world but his sweet voice.

Back in my lounge chair, I feverishly begin to empty my heart in my journal. I'm being summoned yet again for a sand burial! I will lay my pen down once more!

I praise God for the life I now live, a life so much better than I ever dreamed. After twenty years, I can laugh, I can love, and I can enjoy peace and pleasure, even bliss at times. The damaged little girl is with me always, and my old "friend" Fear is never far. The tears that little girl cried never leave me. I have grieved for her, and her lost innocence. I try not to take a moment of peace or joy for granted, and if I ever do, I immediately feel the panic and the mayhem inside me. But I have learned more frequently to focus on the love and overwhelming joy I have in my life. I have learned to respond in the Spirit and not the flesh where the pain lies. I have learned to respond as the victor and not the victim.

My walk into the past is taxing, even gut wrenching. To remember is to relive. I am discovering how the little girl inside of me survived, and I'm learning how to love her to wholeness. I've tried to answer so many questions. I need to understand how, at a critical time in my life when I was at the very end of my rope, I pulled myself up, one hand at a time, and never, ever let go. I don't know why or how, and the only answer I can find is the grace of God. Even when my hands were blistered with pain, from the river I heard those church bells in the distance reminding me of his ever presence. His Spirit was holding me up, encouraging me onward. The little girl inside me was very resourceful, ultimately choosing to focus on hope.

My Angels

God's love shines through the jewels that are our children, Ashley and Jacob. I've never met such awesome young people; they have encouraged me and filled my soul with joy. They have given me such wonderful memories as a mother and helped me recapture some of my stolen innocence. Through every season we have laughed and enjoyed life. Laughter is magical medicine for the soul.

I walk down the hall and gently shake an angel awake. Big green eyes look up at me with her long, blonde hair tousled over her shoulders. She smiles as she receives her marching orders. "Up and at 'em for church." As this is written, my 13-year-old daughter, Ashley, truly is the most anointed spirit I have ever met. She fills me up. I taste her innocence like a sweet wine. Her presence is intoxicating. She fills my life with an awesome sense of accomplishment. Her beauty transcends her pretty round face and perfectly muscular, thin body. She excels at all she touches, whether it is academics, arts or athletics; it doesn't matter. She is a vision of grace and growl. Her competitive nature keeps her on top. Her biggest competitor lies within. What a miracle!

By God's grace, I've raised a healthy, happy child and kept the garbage of my childhood from bleeding into her life, but it wasn't without intense effort on my part. She truly cares more for others than herself, an extremely rare trait found in a teenager. She has been an anesthetic to my pain, helping me to see I had a purpose for living, a reason to rise above.

Being her Mom has given me a love I've never known. She possesses strength in character that draws people into her own, a strength of caring beyond herself. Her spirit blesses all who are in her presence. At times, she is my mentor, helping me learn to respond to a world by being grounded solidly in spirit and truth. She shows me the innocence I've never known, a purity that I embrace as a precious treasure I've never owned. She is a very special person, indeed, who will bless many in her lifetime. Her deepest desire is to praise God with her whole heart and life

Jacob is my young man who lives to please his Mom. He gives unconditional love that sweeps over me like a warm blanket on a cold night. His smile lifts me to new heights, and his personality ignites laughter. A friend told me the other day, "You can just eat him with a spoon, he's so sweet." Yes, my next reason to live was to mother such an awesome child who keeps me laughing. He has an imagination as big as Jupiter, and ever since he could walk, he could talk you into far-away lands. He can sweep you away on an adventure of the century; all conjured up within his 10 year old imagination that will actually make you think you have left the planet. Drama is his passion and he can command a stage.

He's blessed with a sharp wit and an extensive vocabulary, probably from the hundreds of books he has read. He's also blessed with the cutest round face, biggest green eyes, and dimpled smile that would melt away a stone heart. He has a heart full of love and empathy, always wanting to give either of himself or of his possessions.

There is no greed in his soul, only a desire to please, to give, to share his infectious laughter, and to imagine a world better than we have. Thinking his name makes me grin. To feel his arms around my neck and his kisses on my face redeems the entire male race! He is an anointed young man who lives to spread the love of God. I know my children don't act perfectly all the time, but through my eyes, I see their hearts and their spirits and I am so very proud of them. They are the best of me. They are my innocence.

Special Agent, Phil

How do I even begin to describe my most treasured blessing? My husband, Phil, is my Gabriel. I know without a shadow of a doubt that he is a gift from God who saved me from destruction. His love is an answer to prayer that stitched up the wounds of a thousand moons. He is a man who wrapped me in a coating of love that gave me a security like none I have ever known, a coating that replaced the wax coating of shame I felt as a little girl. His love has been a constant in my life.

When he walked into my life more than twenty years ago, I regarded myself as damaged goods and felt that I would, in turn, damage his life. I fell in love with Phil the minute I laid eyes on him. My stomach flipped, and I wanted to gaze into his eyes for the rest of my life. It's amazing how you truly know love. It's magic, something supernatural, way above the ordinary, and made by God. Love makes you care only for the welfare of the other person; you want to spare them pain and spare them heartache.

I immediately built walls around my heart. The walls went up, because he did not deserve my pain, and the aftermath of all the pain. I didn't possess the basic values to make a relationship work, and I had no role models for making a marriage work. I didn't know honesty; I could barely distinguish truth from lies as they departed my lips. I didn't know trust. I trusted no one and didn't expect anyone to trust me. I didn't know love. I didn't know how to give love or how to receive love. I knew I didn't want the marriage my Mother endured. All I knew was that I so wanted someone in my life to give without taking. I wanted someone in my life to hold me close and make the hurt go away.

Well, I ran, and he chased. I put up walls, and he tirelessly tore them down. I pushed him away, and he pulled me closer. He was willing to love me, to accept my history, and to build a future that would be a one-hundred-eighty-degree departure from my past. He had a tenderness that eased the throbbing pain. He had a patience to live through the agony of healing. I grieved then, and, to this day, I grieve my lost childhood, my lost innocence, and my lost love. He woke me from the nightmares, held me through the nights when I wanted to crawl out of my skin, and calmed me.

I lived on the edge, and the edge felt normal. My twisted inherited values said: "You don't love me unless you hit me. You must yell at me, and louder please. I don't deserve calm." I'd never known calm, and it felt so alien. To me, love was abuse coupled with perverse cruelty. I was brainwashed, lost in the darkness of evil. Chaos was normal. Everyone in my life whom I thought loved me let me down. I put Phil in that cluster undeservingly.

I spent the first few years of our relationship pushing his buttons. I convinced myself he would eventually leave me. He too would let me down, because I never, *ever* thought I could be loved with a love that fought so hard for me. One day the words blurted from his lips and covered me like an electric blanket, "You'll never hurt me enough to make me leave you. I will never leave you, because I love you, and I'm going to love you through this. We'll make it to the other side. Just hold me tight and cry as much as you need to cry." I was in such anguish, but the sleepless nights in his arms crying through the torment put me on the road to recovery. His arms were my cast for the brokenness of my soul.

He is my soul mate, and God gave him the grace and strength to process my repulsive past. God gave me a love that fairy tales are born of and strength to move mountains, one rock at a time. I thank God for every moment of every day.

Phil also suffered from a youth of destruction. An alcoholic mother and an abusive father made for a fog of sadness. He raced to survive, to excel, to leave all the pain behind and run toward a dream. Tormented by memories of a sick mother, a distant father, and raised in poverty, he dealt with pain so differently. Our childhood memories birthed desperation to seek what was foreign to both of us: peace and joy. We wanted a home filled with peace and true joy.

For more than 20 years, Phil has helped me come to know and experience *agape* love. Phil has shown me a love that never quits, that endures, that nurtures and that stands.

We now have a home filled with peace and joy. Yet, for some reason, the battle in me rages on. I don't know why the battle continues to be so fierce in my life. Satan relentlessly fights for me each and every day, and I have to fight tough for the sake of my sanity and happiness. I make a choice to be happy. I stand firm in my faith and this happiness, knowing God has given it to me. It was for this moment in time that I survived death's grip. I survived that dark night of the past, so that I could take Phil's hand and run toward the dream, the one God planted in my heart, the same dream I had wished on every birthday candle and every first star at night.

Soul Mate

To violated women, all men sometimes become the enemy. It is easy to use the filter of abuse to react in relationships with other men. It becomes natural to convince yourself that all men are evil and can't be trusted. This is the root of many failed relationships. It takes a man of true character to love a female who has suffered sexual abuse. It takes a man who knows godly love (*agape*) – a love that is long-suffering, a love that lays down ego, a love that fights and never gives up. It takes a man of humility who wants to listen more than he wants to attempt to fix. It takes a patient love that is outlined in 1 Corinthians 13:6: "Love is patient, love is kind, love suffers long ... love never fails."

God wants us to experience this kind of true love. In order to experience such love, God wants us to forgive the man who hurt us and all men who have the potential to hurt us. When we discover such a man, I think we have found the true meaning of Soul mate. I thank God I have this kind of partner as my husband, a mate who truly knows what my soul needs to be happy.

CHAPTER 20

Coloring My Past

The day is flying by, and I have a lot of business to do with the river. This is my day of deliverance. This is the day in my life that is going to make the difference on my journey to wholeness and healing. This is my mountaintop experience, my bend in the river that I will be able to call my milestone. I begin to pray, "God help me to lift the pressure to achieve great things. Help me to achieve Your will for my life. Help me to recognize Your hand. You have given me the most wonderful man in the world to love me and two beautiful, loving children. You have given me a stable, happy, and secure home life with Phil and those children. I want you to control the drive inside of me, this constant drive to prove something to the world, to earn my worth. Lord, help me be content with today and turn tomorrow over to You."

I see God at this moment, in the rocks, in the wind, in the breathtaking scenery of the waterfalls. I feel the cool mist of the water on my face. I feel His cleansing spirit wash over me. I see His hand of majesty and I feel His power. If only I had a paintbrush. But I know I never could truly capture the essence of sovereignty that surrounds me. I paint this moment in my mind. Painting has become my new hobby. I'm taking art classes and loving it, just like I loved to color as a girl. The paintbrush is a passion in my life, as if I am holding a part of my childhood in my hand.

I can paint the past and the future. I remember desperately wanting to color, desperately wanting to lose myself in my coloring books, but being denied this small childhood pleasure. Through my painting, I can live the joy

I missed and bring back the color and creativity to my world that was so lacking as a child. I can express myself in a way that brings joy to others. I can use my brush to paint what I feel and let those feelings translate on my canvas. For the first time in my life, I have the power to paint my world.

Echoes of Carl

Are we remembered in this life for our worst behavior, our worst day, our worst moment? I think, "Yes, we are" which is all the more reason to live your best every day because one day, someone may look back on your life to remember who you were and how you lived. I try to forgive Carl every day for what he did to me, with the difficulty of forgiving a dead man. I draw strength from what Jesus says in Matthew 5:43-45, "You have heard that it was said, 'You shall love you neighbor and hate your enemy.' But I say to you, love your enemies, bless those who curse you, do good to those who hate you, and pray for those who spitefully use you and persecute you, that you may be sons of your Father in heaven; for He makes His sun rise on the evil and on the good, and sends rain on the just and on the unjust."

My intention is not to destroy the memory of one man, but to identify the characteristics and abuse that plagues many children and renders them helpless. My purpose has been to address the disgusting behavior and bring it out of the closet for all those who have never spoken the truth, who keep the secret sealed. Perhaps there is someone reading this book who is abusing a child. I pray you realize you are murdering the innocence of a child. You are violently robbing that child of their power and their voice. Your

247

criminal actions will have lifelong repercussions to the child. Stop immediately and seek help.

This book represents my reality. To other people, Carl was a different person. To my Mother, he was a husband she loved, who provided for her, despite the abuse she suffered. Though I don't understand this love, it was very real to her, and she took her vows seriously. He was a son, a brother, a friend, and a father. He was the only father I ever knew, and I do owe a debt of gratitude to his memory for feeding me, clothing me and giving me a roof over my head. And there are some few special memories with the sounds of the traffic and smells of the dining room at Levy's Department Store.

We would walk to the fanciest dress shop in town, and walk straight to the elevator where we were greeted by the elevator operator, a short, black man in uniform. He'd close the huge, metal-grid, hinged door and up we'd travel to the third floor, where children's clothing was located. I remember the grinding screeches of the elevator were loud, with lots of metal banging, and we would arrive on the third floor with a bump. We'd stroll off the elevator straight to the prettiest dresses on the rack. I'd spend the day modeling one pretty dress after another, until he'd pick one out.

Carl prided himself on being a hard worker and he taught me how to work so hard, to push myself past my physical limits. He provided for my basic needs and simultaneously depleted my emotional needs. A father's job is to provide safe boundaries in which a child can grow and flourish. A good father reflects Godly leadership for his family. A good father invests the love of God into your life, a love that builds up, a love that nurtures, a love that endures, an innocent love that would never exploit a child. I want to hope there was some good in his life, but at this most essential task, nurturing love, he failed miserably.

I often wonder what took place in his life, in his childhood, which birthed such anger and fueled such bitter abuse. He had six siblings and never talked about his childhood. When we attended his family gatherings, they all looked like good people. He had a failed marriage before he married my Mother.

I pray from this day forward to do whatever I can to expose this silent epidemic of child sexual abuse. Now is the time to focus on the good, the good in me and the good in my childhood. I respected Carl, because he was the only father I knew, but I hated him, and that hatred grew for years and wiped out the last dregs of affection. The emotions of love and hate are so confused because I dared not love him, because that could mean that I would, sickly, love what he did to me. As a child, and even as an adult, those emotions are so very hard to process. I know he was a sick man, sick for a "daddy" to treat a child the way he treated me, and yet, he was the only daddy I ever knew.

Now I don't know how to feel about him. There is no more rage; I left that too on the raging Chattooga. I guess, with no emotion toward him, I labor to digest my emotions in a spirit of forgiveness, finding peace with both him and my Mother. I would add that I, too, must release and forgive my biological father, who has never been a part of my life, though ironically he lives only a short distance from my Mother in Mobile.

My Mother

I think each of us who have faced denial from our Mother's, yearn for their arms to wrap around us and acknowledge the pain we have suffered. I believe it must be the most painful and excruciating realty for my mother to face that I was sexually abused by her husband. When I was a little girl, I tried so hard to protect my mother. I tried to prevent my stepfather's tirades against her and I tried to protect her life by complying with his brutal sexual assaults. His threats against her life and mine were very real and I felt a constant state of responsibility for our safety.

When I disclosed I never expected my mother's denial. I never imagined that she would stand by him and I swallowed that rejection as a personal attack. That day of rejection by my mother was one of the darkest and most debilitating in my journey. I experienced years of isolation in my pain but that day I truly felt all alone. As an adult, I realize now that she was playing out the battered woman syndrome, controlled by debilitating fear, and mentally incapable of accepting responsibility for my safety. I spent much of my young adulthood and into middle age playing tug-a-war with our relationship wanting desperately to have a close mother-daughter relationship conditioned upon my mother accepting my history of abuse and her responsibility. I would try to have an open and honest relationship, be met with rejection and pull back. I always had great expectations that I could say something that would open her eyes and receive that long awaited response of sympathy and remorse. She on the other hand wanted me to forget and move on. I tried to forgive her but failed miserably because my forgiveness was conditioned. My forgiveness was unconsciously conditioned upon her accepting responsibility for my abuse. God had a great lesson to teach me and it was only through years of resentful and tumultuous times that always ended in tears, the silent treatment or worse, hurtful words spoken in anger that I finally gave up.

God wanted to teach me the lesson of forgiveness through His grace to forgive fully. This forgiveness is to be given freely, unconditionally, with no expectations of reward, of accountability, of apologies, of responsibility. I once heard how toxic unforgiveness was in an analogy that living in unforgiveness is like ingesting poison and expecting the other person to die. I was definitely poising myself. I was playing the "if" game. If my mother would just wrap her arms around me and tell me how sorry she is, and show compassion for the pain I suffered, then I could truly heal. I was continuing to feed my spirit with resentment and anger when my mother continued to respond to me with denial. I wanted my mother to sympathize with my pain and that would have only provided temporary relief but nothing short of total and complete forgiveness can procure lasting release. To be very transparent a part of me wanted to punish her for not responding in a way that met my expectations. I was hateful at times with sudden disrespectful outbursts and then quietly sulking with a bitter heart at others. After years of disappointment, I began to pray for God to change my heart and my response to my mother. I prayed to forgive by His grace and by His power and truly to love my mother as God loves her. I finally learned from God's word that forgiveness is not conditional. I learned that my healing depends on my actions. My focus is no longer on "me" but on how I can be a blessing to my mother and now help her to heal.

When I was in college I received a note written on a "Things To Do" notepad, and it read:

"I wish everything was different. I do not know how to fix it; I only know I love you."
(Signed) Your Mother

I stuck that note in my bible and read often wanting it to say, *"I am sorry you hurt and sorry for the part I played in allowing your pain."* I know now that that was her attempt to say, "I am sorry." I know that she has reached out many times in the best way that she knew how to convey her sympathy. Because it did not come in the ways I wanted, I rejected those efforts and judged her harshly.

It was God's prefect timing where she would face in public our past of sexual abuse. In May of 2010, my mother accepted an invitation to a fashion show where I was to speak and VOICE was being honored. In her excitement to attend the fashion show, I don't think she really processed the impact of seeing VOICE exhibited and coming face to face with this book. Her first response was to run and hide, but she found the courage to stand by my side as my mother. Since that moment, God has continued to heal her heart and help her face our past. God blessed the years I spent praying for God to change my heart and in the process He touched her heart. My prayers are being answered day by day as slowly she is accepting my mission to speak out as an attack on incest and not as an attack on her. My mother loves me and supports my mission to help survivors heal and to help save the next generation of children from suffering the violation of sexual abuse.

The most recent note I received said,

"I am so proud of you and the work you are doing with VOICE."

(Signed) Your Mother

CHAPTER 21

Lord of the River

The river has been cathartic for my soul. I pack my suitcase, saying goodbye to my wee room at the quaint bed and breakfast and the old frayed patchwork quilt that hangs over the daybed. I'm going home a changed person, delivered from the undertow of incest that bound me and rendered me defeated. I claim the victory that God has given me to survive, the strength that He has placed in my life to accept His truth. I say my goodbyes to the river. Its song is the same. Its beauty and power remain strong and steadfast.

I climb into my green Explorer with the excitement and anticipation of seeing my family and having them see the change in me. I stop at the old, red rusted iron bridge. I press the gas lightly to reflect, hearing the thunderous roll under my tires, clanking loudly. When I cross over the bridge, I pull over for one last goodbye. I get out and take one more look around, at the beauty and safety and serenity of God's glory. Will I still feel this way tomorrow? Will I still have the strength to persevere next week, or the week after, or the week after that?

I instinctively pull the ring from my pocket. I look at its sparkling stones, the sapphires and diamonds, still as beautiful as it was that morning when I pulled it out of my Christmas stocking. I had thought the answer was to throw it into the Chattooga River, but I couldn't bring myself to do it, even after several attempts. For some reason, I couldn't release it. For years, it sat in my jewelry box, silently waiting.

I fall to my knees. I lean my forehead on the cold iron metal and look down at the river flowing below. Then I heard it.

"Listen."

It was as if someone spoke to my soul. Deep cries to deep. I've never felt a stronger presence of the Lord. I knew this voice belonged to Him. With my mind washed clean, I obeyed, and I heard this:

"I was there with you and my heart broke for you. I never wanted you to feel the pain, the confusion, the desperation. I love you, Angela, and I was there with you. I've felt your pain every day, I've touched your hurts. I was in the hot car when you gasped for air, I was in the bedroom when he touched you wrongly, I was in the cold sewer in the rain, I was in the bathtub bleeding with you, I was there to open the car door moments before you crossed over to meet Me the night you swallowed the pills, I was in the room when your truth was denied by your mother. I was there the morning you had to move into your car. I'm here with you now. I was also there the day you looked into Phil's eyes and found true love. I was there when Ashley turned blue after birth and I heard your prayers, I was there when Jacob first called you "Mommy" and I was here to deliver you. I don't want you to hurt anymore. I will be here for every tear, every smile, every triumph and every failure. I will never leave you nor forsake you."

I suddenly remember a scripture the Holy Spirit had spoken to me during the depths of my healing process, and I have held it so close to my heart ever since. As God told Israel in Isaiah 54:11, "O you afflicted, storm tossed and not comforted, behold, I will set your stones in fair colors, and lay your foundations with sapphires." At that moment, I knew that my sorrows had been turned into sapphires.

Like a kiln in the fire that burns a rough rock into a beautiful sapphire, my pain and suffering have been the fire, and from that has emerged an abundance of beautiful sapphires.

I put the ring on my finger. And surprisingly, those same feelings that were attached years ago are no longer there. Now the sapphires hold a different meaning. The eight sapphires sparkle victory, not defeat; the diamonds emit perseverance, not vacillation. It is the same ring, but I am a different person. Looking at it now, it becomes a discovery woven into the web of circumstances, a treasure of my resolve. The ring has so much to tell, so much to reveal. This isn't just any sapphire ring. It is a symbol of a turning point and many revelations, a symbol of a path that God has had me on for so long ... a symbol of victory!

I get in my car and slowly drive away. In the rear view mirror, I see the river, the inn, and the bridge disappearing from view. I quickly catch a glimpse of my reflection in the rear view mirror and smile. The sapphires sit perfectly on my finger, sparkling in the sunlight, perched on the steering wheel. As I make my way home, I turn up the volume of my CD, breathe deeply and let the lyrics become my creed:

> From the mountains to the valleys,
> From the rivers to the sea.
> Every hand that reaches out.
> Every hand that reaches out to offer peace.
> Every simple act of mercy.
> Every step to kingdom come.
> All the hope in every hope in every heart
> Will speak what love has done.
> For as long as I shall live I will testify to love.
> I'll be the witness in the silences when

words are not Enough. With every
breath that I take I will Give thanks to
God above.
For as long as I shall live I will testify.
I will testify to love.[12]

On my voyage down the river, I felt such a unity with
nature and a unity with all that is good and pure in this
world. Because of that, I am now able to see and appreciate
so much beauty around me, such blessings in life, and most
importantly, the beauty that lies within me.

I am on a pathway to total peace and joy, with
good days and bad, as I walk through my pain. Satan
will try to use my past to paralyze me, but I must
stand firm in Christ to render him powerless. As God
has a plan for my life, so does Satan. I commit to
God's plan, and I rebuke Satan and the evil he has
brought into my life. Sometimes, I have to say many
times in a day, "Satan, get thee behind me." Some
days I have to pray without ceasing. Some days I
simply have to stand firm. Some days I fail, and I
pledge to try harder tomorrow, but regardless, I know
that God is with me ... always.

In recounting the events of my life and committing
them to these pages, I had time to reflect and recall
how much I've been blessed with support and
inspiration to dig deeper and reveal the conscious and
subconscious turmoil inside me.

I have come to accept my true nature in Christ as
good and not evil. Even though I was surrounded by
evil as a child, I know that Carl's evil did not invade
my being. My spirit is not filled with the evil of my

experiences, which have been poured out at the foot of the cross. My strong will, even in the face of extreme cruelty and persistent criticism, was birthed from this spirit.

Some days this will is a curse, never wanting to accept failure or defeat, but on many days, I see it as a gift from God. This determination to survive, to succeed, gives me an edge, one that seems to be a magnet to people who are also survivors. God has blessed me with special people to love me through this pain, people of strong spirit and strong character and a tremendous capacity to love.

Through them, I have learned that to give is to receive, to bless is to be blessed. I also learned that, with the determination to surrender totally to God and His will, a way is found. Ugliness engulfed me for so long, but no more. The evil *events* of my past are purged from my life forever, and I stopped the curse: I chose not to become a monster. God chose to save me. He called, and I answered. He has given me a gift to touch people through my life, through the people I love, and hopefully through this writing. I accept that gift and pray He will use it to further His glory.

The Other Side of Grace

I am so desperate for the fairy-tale ending, so committed to remain sane and to be happy. Yet in this book, I am pledged to total transparency. As I put this book on public record, I will put it there knowing, for the first time in my life, I have done something that totally discloses the essence of my childhood experience of sexual abuse, and the turbulence that steered my soul. I still struggle with the abuse and its

258

effects. I have turned it over to God a million times, and I'm learning on my journey that total surrender is the key. I have to keep turning it over, and maybe that's where God wants me, humble and needing Him so desperately to make it through to the other side of grace.

It is a two-fisted struggle: One to fight depression, one to fight perfectionism. I battle both with everything in me. Not that I think I'm perfect for a second, but I want my world perfect, and I don't feel like people will love me unless I strive to be perfect; and it is that compulsion for perfection and approval that I must fight every day. I want my husband to be perfect, my children perfect, my home perfect, my office perfect, my company perfect ... I set such high expectations for everything in my life that it can be hard to function in my world. It is very difficult for those who love me to put up with me. I fight these compulsions, and I wonder if they stem from the "perfect house" my Mother demanded and the "perfect image" my stepfather commanded. I fight those ideas.

I fight for my stability on a daily basis because I am worth it; Christ died for me! Some days I'm so strong, and some days I just want to curl up in a ball and pull the covers over my head, and say, "Forget it, I'm tired of fighting."

I wish I could carve out the malignant memories I've exposed and throw them away, like digging your fingers inside a Halloween pumpkin to rip out the guts and seeds. I wish this had never happened to me. I wish I could quit trying to have all the right answers. I know God is sovereign, and I know He loves me. I am healing. The healing process is a journey. I faced this challenge for myself, and my prayer is that this telling will help others to face theirs and to find in God a sure and true Healer.

CHAPTER 22

The King's Ring

When something supernatural happens, the secular world tries to explain it away as coincidence. When something supernatural happens to me, I fall to my knees in praise with no words to utter. As the original ring was given by Carl to purchase my silence, God recently gave me a new *sapphire ring* to affirm my voice! Can you believe it? The giver, Judy Overton, had only met me two months before. The costly eight-sapphire ring had been bought for her by her husband! But she felt, without telling me, that God was saying she should give it to *me*!

"At choir practice," she said, "the voice got so loud in my head that I could not deny it was God." She felt compelled to obey. Judy had witnessed some of my stress, but I never told her explicitly why I was struggling. Amazingly, Judy heard a voice in her head say, "Angela needs this ring *to affirm her ministry.*"

While I was out, she came to my office to give it to me and then returned the next day, determined to find me. Hours before, while dropping off a watch to be repaired, I had been trying on sapphire rings at a jewelry store. When she handed me the ring, I was overwhelmed with emotion. I was astonished that God would move Judy to give me such a ring.

She was determined to put it on my finger, no matter how many times I repeated that I couldn't take such an extravagant gift. She had never read the book and had no idea what a sapphire ring meant to me in my journey of healing! Her gift, twice the size of my original ring, displays a large marquis solitaire sapphire in the middle, surrounded by sapphire baguettes and a crown of diamonds on top and bottom. It is so stunning I can't imagine any woman giving it away. Her husband supported her.

What an awesome God we serve! Not because He gave me a spectacular sapphire ring, but because He chose to touch me in such a personal way. He knows how emotionally difficult my task is going to be to speak out on incest. I had been in a constant state of prayer over this book and how to accomplish the very clear, long-range assignment He has given me. I believe He wanted me to have a constant reminder on my hand that He is right here with me, and only through His power can I begin a movement to help shed light and understanding on incest.

Recently God assured me I don't have to fear anymore. I was physically holding on to the pain. I was allowing my old friend Fear to stay too close for too long. God revealed this in me during a weeklong body detoxification, fasting, meditation and relaxation. Now I know that my body is the temple of the Holy Spirit, and I am to treat it as such. The scared little girl is now a strong and determined woman on a mission. I have released the fear in my life, and I embrace the challenge set before me with courage and great anticipation.

CHAPTER 23

Rally Cry for Innocence

VOICE: Victory Over Injustice Changes Everyone

Various popular causes are poised front and center in the public awareness arena, daily gaining support and resources. Look at their colors: red speaks for AIDS victims and for heart disease; green screams at us to "save the environment; "pink is the voice of breast cancer, the disease that attacks one in eight women.

Yet one of every four women has experienced *child sexual abuse*; it is a hushed, bitter and damaging sore in their hearts. The same is true for one in six men. With these combined statistics, however, only one out of every ten will ever tell another living soul about a child sexual abuse experience. It is now high time for *the color white* to be launched.

Our society has faced many taboo's head on ---teen pregnancy, homosexuality, and the AIDS epidemic to name a few. I am one voice dressed in white fighting for the innocence of children, praying that the blanket of darkness over this last taboo will be lifted, and the captives who scream silently will be set free. I wear white when I speak in public as a banner to promote prevention of child sexual abuse, the protection of innocent children and the healing of those traumatized by sexual abuse. Child sexual abuse is not a popular cause, not an easy battle, and certainly not comfortable topic for public conversation. It is an intense issue with no easy answers. I pray for the day when millions worldwide will wear white as a sign of unity and solidarity to stop child sexual abuse and together work to remove the stigma of child sexual abuse from the victim.

The foundations of love and trust are destroyed when an adult exploits a child for the purpose of personal sexual gratification. Not only is the child ravaged physically and injured emotionally, but he or she is also trapped in silence and destined to bear these heavy burdens alone. The pain, confusion, guilt, and grief that torment the child scream on into adulthood and bleed into the lives of everyone associated with a survivor. Ninety percent of abuse is inflicted by someone the child knows, loves and trusts; consequently, the child remains silent about the sexual abuse. There is a warped manipulation that grooms the child into silence. Family members so often know the abuser but turn a blind eye. The majority of disclosures of abuse are met with denial when the child is discredited, shut down, or ignored. The protection of the abuser is often more important than care and justice for the child.

It is stunning to listen to the hundreds of accounts when survivors finally speak of their abuse and to the horrific responses of family and friends. Rather than receiving a compassionate and nurturing response, the child is frequently confronted with panic, denial, anger, and containment. The child is left to navigate this trauma, feeling totally at fault and damaged.

Despite these challenges, the crusade must be waged with unlimited and unyielding commitment and energy. There have been many crusaders throughout history who have fought for justice. My dream is that this injustice and injury against children be stopped. My dream is that children's innocence, currently held captive by ignorance, arrogance and denial, will be protected. It is time that children are freed from the threat and risk of ongoing sexual abuse caused by an uneducated and apathetic society. Adults must be willing to learn and be trained, and then commit to being vigilant about prevention and protection. *Darkness To Light (D2L.org)* provides this opportunity in their training that educates adults on the issue and how to prevent child sexual abuse.

The color white is a perfect iconic focus for the protection of the innocence of children and the prevention of child sexual abuse. Innocence is precious and preserves a child's right to be a child and face normal emotional, physical and spiritual development, undefiled by the evil of sexual abuse. White is a color that honors innocence. White doves are a symbol of innocence and peace; a bride wears white as a symbol of purity. White diamonds, white horses, white snow–all of these speak to goodness, purity, and innocence.

Child sexual abuse, on the contrary, puts a deep dark whole in the spirit of a child, opening the door to an ocean of desperation and deceit. This abuse turns promise into peril, trust into fear and innocence into self-destruction. It heaps guilt and shame on a tender spirit and leads the child into isolation and silence. Love, sex, trust, and boundaries are all distorted with little, if any, to no support, to help the victim sort through these damaging emotions. There are no words to describe the damage of child sexual abuse on a child's life. There are no words, other than His own, to describe how serious an issue this is to God: *"Whoever receives a child in my name receives me, but whoever causes one of these little ones to stumble it would be better to have a millstone tied around their neck and drowned in the depth of the sea." Matthew 18:5-6.* I have launched WHITE OUT CHILD SEXUAL ABUSE DAY on April 30th to encourage the wearing of white to honor victims of child sexual abuse.

My calling is to make this verse come to life in every adult by opening eyes wide to the huge, undeniable responsibility God places on adults to prevent a child from stumbling. This dream has been nurtured in *VOICE Today*, a faith-based non-profit organization founded to minister healing to victims of child sexual abuse and provide prevention resources.

The VOICE Movement is an awareness campaign designed to educate society on the risk of and response to child sexual abuse. Our world exhibits great signs of deliberate denial of the crisis. Child sexual abuse statistics vary from country to country and public reports are inconsistent at best. However, they are alarming, especially when one considers that the numbers are believed to be vastly understated. One country's research indicates that up to 36% of girls and 29% of boys have suffered child sexual abuse; another study reveals up to 46% of girls and 20% of boys have experienced sexual coercion (The 57th session of the UN Commission on Human Rights[10]). When 30% or more children are sexually abused worldwide, we are facing an epidemic of unspeakable proportions and we must seek answers. Child sexual abuse also crosses every social, ethnic and economic boundary. One child sexually violated is too many; millions violated is totally unacceptable. It is time for a major movement of protection and prevention, which the VOICE Movement is now launching.

The VOICE Movement is growing as mighty warriors seek education and training on how to prevent child sexual abuse in their homes, neighborhoods, faith centers, and communities. Once trained, these workers step out as vocal advocates and protectors of children. The VOICE Movement also provides a platform for survivors to break their silence with support, encouragement, compassion and empowerment.

Those of us who are survivors of this monstrous evil can never recover a childhood lost to sexual abuse, but there is personal power and great reward in guarding the future of today's children. This focus allows a survivor to find good purpose out of the evil events of their youth. It takes the focus off a survivor's pain and applies it to a noble objective.

There are no easy answers to reverse this generational curse that has plagued society since biblical times. However, we must begin to ask the tough questions. It is time that we expose the arrogance that teaches, "It won't happen in my home," or "My child would tell me" or "Uncle Clarence would never do that." When a child discloses the damage is done, and protection is too late. The child is traumatized and may suffer for years or decades to come. Worse yet, the child won't tell at all and suffers in painful silence and isolation. In either case, manifestation of destructive behaviors that show up during childhood, persist long into adulthood, frequently taking the form of serious character flaws.

Silence is deceit, and silence is the tool the evildoers of this world use to perpetuate this sexual sin. Society is affected by the issues of child sexual abuse: adults who are apathetic, parents who are in denial, families who protect the perpetrators, teachers and other professionals who don't report, churches who don't want to know, the medical community who seeks to treat only physical ailments, taxpayers who fund remediation and incarcerations, survivors who become predators, families and loved ones of victims, and a community that doesn't understand the impact on lives and remains too embarrassed to shed light on this last taboo.

It is an uncomfortable subject but we must wake up to the reality. Unfortunately, the majority of people stand in the depths of denial, blind to the reality around them. Make no mistake: child sexual abuse is everywhere. Even, and especially, the Bible speaks openly of incest and how it was covered up. Read further about the trail of sin of King David and the pain Tamar suffers in 2 Samuel 13. It is astonishing that churches don't openly, enthusiastically and aggressively embrace child sexual abuse prevention and healing by mandating programs for all individuals. With this crisis at epidemic proportion, it is time that all youth serving organizations are trained to prevent, detect and properly respond to child sexual abuse issues. Prevention initiatives need to become viral and the norm of our society rather than the exception. This means that efforts cannot be driven by risk of litigation or liability, but by an overwhelming commitment to protection and safety.

Everyone has the power to intercede, but rarely does anyone act. Once child sexual abuse is revealed, it has an impact on the family for a lifetime. The victim is made to feel responsible for the abuse and to suffer in silence with no recovery support, understanding or encouragement. The victim is also frequently ostracized if they don't maintain their silence. The victim is told to "keep it silent, forget about it and just move on" to protect the perpetrator.

Children remain in isolation destined to navigate life through a filter of betrayal that is beyond comprehension for the non-survivor. It is no wonder that substance abuse, anger, depression, promiscuity, suicide, relational struggles, and criminal behaviors are among the numerous social ills rampant in our society. Moral issues become very confusing for the victim: The message to simply "move on with your life" desecrates the virginity of children and makes it easier for the victim to "excuse, look away, move on" from the next moral failure -- until some end up in the gutters of human degradation. First, there is a failure of moral courage from those in a position to protect the child at the time the crime is exposed. Then the victim watches and keeps score: Mom didn't act; Dad didn't act; the family didn't act; the minister didn't act; the police were never called; and no counselor ever intervened. These adult failures and lack of understanding, compassion and justice further traumatize the survivor. The abuse adversely affects personal growth and development and the lives of those surrounding the victim, who struggle with the stigma and accountability. The death of innocence is the birth of rage. The loss of power is the birth of fear.

What is the child to conclude but that: "I and my body are not of value to any of the significant people in my life, and I am responsible to maintain peace in our home by keeping quiet and covering up the egregious act."

Surely, God weeps when He witnesses this evil.

The consequences to children and society begin immediately. The Darkness to Light Foundation reports that child sexual abuse is a direct source of many serious problems facing society today. Here are some of the foundation's new measurements of the full societal impact of sexual abuse:

1. 70-80% of sexual abuse survivors report excessive drug and alcohol use.
2. One study showed that among male survivors, 50% have suicidal thoughts and more than 20% attempt suicide.
3. Young girls who are sexually abused are more likely to develop eating disorders as adolescents.
4. More than 60% of teen first pregnancies are preceded by experiences of molestation, rape or attempted rape.
5. The average age of the offenders is 27 years old.
6. Approximately 40% of sex offenders report sexual abuse as children.
7. Both males and females who have been sexually abused are more likely to engage in prostitution.

8. Approximately 70% of sexual offenders of children have between 1 and 9 victims; 20-25% has 10 to 40 victims.
9. Serial child molesters may have as many as 400 victims in their lifetimes.

For survivors, the path to recovery starts with reclaiming their voices and speaking out. There is power in numbers. There are estimated 42,000,000 to as high as 60,000,000 reported adult survivors in the U.S. If only a *portion* of them were to take a stand and join The VOICE Movement, we could bring about important social change. This social change can set victims free, and can add new levels of vigilance and determination to our efforts to prevent child sexual abuse and can protect the lives of children in the next generation. You can champion this change by joining The VOICE Movement by demanding prevention programs be taught in your communities, your faith centers and other youth serving organizations!

A child needs a plan of protection. Parents can instill that plan as suggested by many child advocates. Parents can teach a child about his or her personal power, personal boundaries and about inappropriate touch. They can implement that plan with three basic messages: Saying "NO," RUNNING, and TELLING.

1. Teach children their loud, guttural, forceful and powerful "NO" voices. Give them permission to say "NO" to unwanted or uncomfortable behavior, affection, touch or visual images.
2. Teach children to RUN with urgency out of an uncomfortable situation if someone is

trying to invade their personal boundaries, or force affection upon them.

3. Teach children to TELL exactly what has happened to the first person they see. If a child tells someone who does not believe them, teach them that you will always believe them, and that it is your job to protect them. They must tell until someone believes them.

In addition to giving your child the right to say no, what else can I do, you ask?

1. Teach your child safe personal boundaries.
2. Monitor one-on-one time with adults. Drop in unexpectedly and ask how the visit went.
3. Learn to ask a difficult but vital question: **"Has anyone ever touched your private parts?"**
4. Monitor on-line internet use and keep computers in a central public location.
5. Listen for non-verbal signs and recognize distinct behavioral changes.
6. Believe your child and report offenders; child sexual abuse is a crime.

Even today, if you have ever been sexually abused as a child, and have never spoken of it, *tell someone now. Speak out!* The secret holds power over you until it is released. You deserve to heal; you deserve to live a life of peace and joy. If you are a child being abused, tell a trusted adult or friend. If you suspect a child is being sexually abused, get

involved; don't turn your back on a helpless child. Don't send the message that no-one cares. Don't fear the consequences. Call 911 and report the crime immediately.

Few individuals know how to protect their children from sexual abuse, and even fewer know how to respond compassionately to a survivor. *I am often asked if the problem is escalating, and the answer is yes.* Online pornography is increasing the appetite for younger and younger children. Predators are prowling social networking sites and chat rooms finding easy access to a vulnerable child. Child-on-child abuse is on the rise as children are acting out the pornography they view online, compounding an already horrific epidemic.

Worldwide corruption is rampant and the exploitation of children is quickly replacing drugs as an industry, a reusable commodity being bought and sold, and devoured like a loaf of bread. As poverty grows, parents are selling children to provide for the family. In some countries, mothers don't even realize they are selling their children into the sex industry when they are offered money for them to work in America. Mothers send their children off willingly, believing there are giving them a chance for a better life. Education and awareness has to be urgently shared.

The evil of child sexual abuse and child sexual exploitation is gaining ground every day. We don't have a second to lose. These children who are being trafficked need a message of healing and love; they need to know that they are cherished, no matter what they have been forced to do. But they also need our help to escape this fate.

My rally cry is simple: Please help us protect the next generation of children. Join The VOICE Movement to help eradicate this horrid injustice that is affecting millions of children by helping them regain their Voices and supporting the education of the adults around them.

Please help open the box of hidden secrets of child sexual abuse borne by men, women and children today. Help them stand up honestly and courageously without shame or fear by listening to their hearts and validating their voices. Please give of your time, your talents and your resources to help end child sexual abuse and survivors heal. Stand with us in The VOICE MOVEMENT and break the silence and cycle of child sexual abuse.

ACKNOWLEDGMENTS

First, and foremost, I thank God for being so very good to me, in answering the prayers of my heart and turning my sorrows into sapphires. He brought me through a time of awful humiliation, but He assured me that in His eyes I was a precious jewel. It was His love that transformed me from a broken vessel of ridicule and shame into the whole and healed woman I am today. All praise and glory goes to Him and Him alone.

I thank my husband and family for giving of their time in sacrifice to help me in this battle.

I so appreciate Jan and Bruce Willson of Hopehouse Inc. in Maine for her healing theme song and her encouragement of the VOICE ministry.

I am so blessed that I had not one, not two, not three but hundreds of angels who went before me and with me to develop this book. I wish I could list every single one. I know they join me in prayer for the total and complete healing of family abuses for each person who turns these pages.

Caroline Friday is an amazing woman of faith and creative talent. I begged her to read the first pages and tell me if I should keep going. Her response was, "You must," and she became a tremendous mentor and prayer partner who gave countless hours of time and energy to the project.

Michael Richardson is definitely my most valuable player on this project. Such a man of prayer, praise and power, a man gifted with discernment to hear God's voice that this was his mission to touch the book, and touch he did in an amazing way. I appreciate his ability to turn my bleeding on the pages into an account that will change lives. He also stood in the gap as a surrogate father here on earth, giving me those gentle pats on the back that I yearned for from my own father.

I thank Liza Scales for bringing a fresh set of eyes in reviewing and improving this manuscript.

All my precious friends and confidantes – you know who you are – have my undying gratitude. I also want to acknowledge all the women, children, sadly also, men and boys who have suffered childhood sexual abuse. Be brave, speak up, get help and start to forgive with each page of life you turn. Surrender to the pain, talk and then heal. It will take great faith, in God and in yourself, but by all means tell your story. Be strong, and tell it!

I celebrate His work in me with my daily companion – the following song and its lyrics by Jan Willson:

> *From sorrows to sapphires …*
> *On these, rebuild my life.*
> *For years, so much fire …*
> *Now Lord, make stones that shine!*
> *Do whatever is required*
> *For You to turn those times*
> *From sorrows to sapphires…*
> *Your foundation for my life!* [11]

APPENDIX

Signature Sapphires

Sapphires mean so much to me because my Father God has chosen them as living lights and symbols of His precious love and grace to me. The first sapphire ring I was given didn't do much for me, but the sapphires themselves always have spoken to my heart. When God audibly spoke to my spirit on that iron bridge years ago about the treasured stones, they have continued to multiply in my life. Shame on me for attempting to throw the sapphire ring away and deny its true beauty, which comes from God. Shame on me also for attempting to throw my life away, and for not seeing my own beauty. When God gave me a second and superior ring, again sapphires, it simply amazed me. I prayed for affirmation, and it came: a greater sapphire ring.

Let me tell you about all my sapphires. They are treasures in their "royal hue." Mined from underground, they form under intense pressure and fire that expose their beauty. Some sapphires are delivered from the fire too early, never to reach their full, sparkling potential, never to gain their true beauty. Others endure intense heat in excess of 3000 C to bring out the most vibrant blue, true beauty. Then even more polishing is required to reveal their true color and luster.

They are not only a precious stone for their amazing beauty but also for their amazing strength. They can be transformed from beautiful gemstones to transparent crystal slices and used as watch faces in high quality watches, as their exceptional hardness makes the face almost impossible to scratch. Just so, the surface of incest is hard to scratch and virtually impossible to break through.

The sapphires hold secrets much like an abused child – hidden resources of strength and inner beauty. The surface of sapphires may be hard to scratch, much like the hardened inner core of an abused child. The secret in the sapphire is sometimes never revealed, much like the real beauty in an abused child. The secret of the abuse is buried so far down in the soul of a child that it sometimes takes a lifetime to mine the secret, heat the secret to 3000 C to purify the hurt, and polish the soul. Even as the earth's crust contaminates the precious sapphire stone, so does the violation of abuse contaminate the soul of the child. The impurities of the hurt have to be purged by the heat, which can seem unbearable.

Yet so often, the pain is suffered in silence because no one else is in the intense heat with you. When the polishing begins to remove the impurities, to remove the intense pain, it sometimes takes years for the true beauty to shine. Sometimes, the abuse makes the surface extremely hard to scratch, so that more pain won't filter into the heart of the stone. The hard surface helps the stone survive, much like the abused child who is admonished to protect everyone from the secret.

When at their best, sapphires, as gemstones, stand out in excellence. They create unique ambience whether in a ring or other displays. More than anything, someone has thought about a sapphire a long time before anyone sees it. I know God has turned my sorrows to sapphires.

Let me tell you about symbolism in my sapphires. Ironically, there are eight of them, just as there are eight baguettes of sapphires in the King's Ring given to me. I love it when God kisses you on the cheek and says I am right here!

ω Sapphire 1: A Christ-Centered Life

Receiving Christ, trusting Christ, surrendering to Christ as my Lord and Savior is my lifeline. Christ has sustained me and continues to sustain me through every day. The love of Jesus has healed much pain. It is a supernatural love and comfort that held me, and holds me, in the darkest of nights. I am on a voyage of healing. Some days I think I can do it all on my own, as I tried so hard to do for so many years. The abuse in my childhood makes me retreat into my hurt. I am sometimes as a Styrofoam cup punctured with holes; in these times, it is as if my soul cannot hold His love. It seeps out.

I sometimes put an enormous amount of pressure on myself to complete the impossible. I heard a wonderful man speak, Art Berg, who said, "The possible takes time; the impossible just takes a little longer." So I am learning to be patient with myself. The little girl inside me had to work hard as a child to earn approval, to earn a kind word, to earn a hug, and such old patterns die hard. I found it impossible to receive, not only to receive the love of Christ, but also to receive the love of my husband, my children, and the love of friends. I always feel as though I have to earn every bit of goodness in my life. I didn't know how to fill myself; I didn't know how to receive. It still is very hard for me to receive. I love very deeply, I'm a giver, and I get my feelings hurt easily. I'm learning to create boundaries. And the process continues as I hold God's hand, and I know He holds mine.

Trust is a noun and trust is a verb. I believed in the noun and not the verb. I knew what trust was, and logically, I could recite my faith, my belief, and my eternal hope. What I didn't know was how to reach my arms straight up to the sky and say, "Take me Lord. Take my life and make it Yours, take my heart, take my mind, take my body, take my family, take my belongings, take my business, take my pain, take my past, take it all and give me…You." Take this world and give me Jesus. We have to pour out our whole self to Him; we have to give Him EVERYTHING!

I struggled with who God was in my life. I struggled with fear of God, as I feared Carl. I struggled with fear of abandonment by God because my biological father had left me, turning his back on me. I had no concept of who God was in my life, and no concept of how much he loved me. When I heard the words "God the Father," or "Our Father who art in heaven," or "Abba Father," I conjured images of the only earthly fathers I had known.

Through God's Word, through Godly people, and through my quiet time, I had to introduce myself to my heavenly Father. I had to fall in love with Him. I had to learn to trust Him. I had to forgive Him. I was angry. He could have delivered me from the abuser; He could have stopped the abuse. He is God. I had to forgive HIM. It has been a fight.

Like trust, control is a noun and control is a verb. Control has been my stronghold, as trust has been my weakness. The little girl who cries inside of me never had control, and once I got control of my life, I abused that control. I wanted to control my life and everyone in it. I wanted a perfect life created from unrealistic expectations of myself and everyone else in my world. I know God does not want this. He is our creator, and He wants control of His creation for His purposes. We are mere humans.

Through my journey, Jesus has drawn me closer and closer to Himself. He takes me to places of surrender and re-surrender. Receiving His love, surrendering to His will, and especially trusting Him have been most difficult. Jesus loves like no other. The poison in my life left me with an ungodly shame that resulted in self-hatred. I didn't feel worthy, never good enough for God. I had to accept that Jesus' love is so much greater than my self-hatred and rejection. It took a very long time to surrender to His love, a very long time to accept the gift of grace.

I cling to Psalm 139:13, "For you created my inmost being; you knit me together in my Mother's womb." I still battle the demons of unworthiness and shame, but now I consider those feelings as lying whispers from the enemy of our souls. Shame without respite leads to feeling as if I'm never good enough. Every victory He gives me makes me stronger. Had I not experienced such pain in my life, I would not have experienced the healing power of Christ, who is the promised sapphire. My healing is a journey of receiving, a journey of trust, and a journey of surrender.

ω *Sapphire 2: Forgiveness*

Forgiveness is hard. Let's face it, isn't it easier to be angry? The flesh is weak, but in the power of the spirit, we find forgiveness. Forgiveness is a supernatural act. Our flesh wants justice, accountability, validation, and answers. I learned that forgiveness is not an option, but an act of obedience. The only thing keeping me from obedience in Christ was selfish fear. I didn't believe Jesus would do what He said He would do if I obeyed Him. I didn't know that my forgiveness would produce peace. I learned from God's Word that unforgiveness was a yoke around my neck, a costly burden. I also learned that forgiveness was for my benefit and my benefit alone. Whether others deserved my forgiveness was not for me to decide. I learned in God's word to obey God and forgive.

Forgiveness brought *me* peace. Peace with God is peace with yourself. God promises His peace. He does not promise us a life free from trials and tribulation, but He does promise us peace. Justice is in God's hands, not ours. "If it is possible, as much as it depends on you, live peaceably with all men. Beloved, do not avenge yourselves, but rather give place to wrath, for it is written, 'Vengeance
is mine, I will repay,' says the Lord." (Romans 12:18-19).

In my walk, I learned that the forgiveness we give actually flows from the forgiveness we receive from God. That lesson hit home, because all too often I stumble. I sin, and when I fail miserably, I can stand before my Lord, confess, ask for forgiveness, and repent of my sinful ways. I had to learn to forgive God, to forgive my Mother, Carl, my biological father, my grandparents - anyone and everyone who I felt turned and looked away from my suffering. I learned that God didn't cause my abuse, but like the biblical character Job, he allowed it, perhaps so that I could experience this deliverance I have and share it with others (this suggestion is in 2 Cor. 1:3). I learned to forgive and forgive and forgive, until at times, I couldn't breathe. Then I had to walk away and forgive some more. I believe that we have to get to the point in life where we can say, "What you did deeply wounded me, but I no longer hold you responsible. Christ paid your debt."

As I walk out my faith, I walk out forgiveness. The following prayer has really helped me. It comes from Andy Comiskey's *Living Waters Study Book:*

Prayer of Forgiveness

"Father, even as You have freely forgiven me, I choose to release _____ unto You. I forgive _____ for sinning against me. I forgive _____ specifically for sinning against me in these ways. (Name them specifically.) I ask in turn that Your Sovereign grace and justice would come to bear upon _____ (the wounder). Be Lord over _____, even as I ask You to become Lord and Healer over my wounded heart. Continue to heal my heart, even as You bring up the residual emotions and reactions not yet wholly known to me. Help me quickly to face these realities at the foot of the Cross, knowing that I have forgiven, but am still being healed." I ask that you recite this prayer and find forgiveness.

ω *Sapphire 3: Prayer*

Prayer is my aspirin. Prayer is a pain reliever that eases my suffering. Prayer is the medicine of healing. Prayer is always my answer when I can't breathe, can't live, can't forgive, can't smile, can't put one foot in front of another; I must pray. Prayer is my power source that energizes me beyond my own potential. When I speak to God, He answers me, He comforts me, and He calms my fears. When I seek Him, I find Him. I feel His presence. God answers prayer. I prayed and prayed and wished on every birthday candle for a happy family. I prayed for healing, I prayed for strength, I prayed to forgive, I prayed for joy, and I pray without ceasing all throughout my day. God answers prayer. Overcome evil with good - pray. God tells us to pray without ceasing. (1 Thess. 5: 17)

"Be still and know I am God." He wants us to quiet our spirits and hear from Him. He not only wants us to talk to Him but He wants to speak to us. So pray and listen!

ω *Sapphire 4: Reconciliation for Love*

Love is the most precious gift in the world. Love heals, love fills, and love pulls you up by your bootstraps. If not for the love in my life, I would not live. God has filled my heart with love that overflows. He has taught me to love Him and to love myself, which is a challenge. It took years to find myself – who I really was inside – and to love that person unconditionally. It took forgiveness to love. It took getting it right within myself so I could love others. You can't give what you don't have; you can't love others if you don't love yourself. When you love yourself, you learn to give love that comes back to you in volumes. I have been blessed to find the love of a soul mate, the most precious love designed by God. A love that "suffers long and is kind, does not envy, does not parade itself, is not puffed up, does not behave rudely, does not seek its own, is not provoked, thinks no evil, does not rejoice in iniquity but rejoices in the truth, bears all things, believes all things, hopes all things, endures all things; a love that never fails." (1 Cor. 13:4-6)

The love of my children has filled my heart with a vicarious childhood, a love that fills corners of my heart that were vacant. The love in my life now has given me courage to dream, to reach out and experience joy. Loving my Mother has made me learn to love when you don't *want* to love. It has taught me to love beyond the hurt, beyond the anger. It has made me understand that love is a command, not a choice. We must always be ready to give love and receive love, the radiant jewel of our lives.

ω *Sapphire 5: Time*

Time is a precious stone. Time passes faster and faster with every year. It is one of the most precious gifts you can give and one of the most precious gifts you can receive. It takes time to nurture relationships, it takes time to grow in your faith, and it also takes time to heal. How do you show someone you love them? One significant way is to spend time with them. God wants us to spend time with Him, time to grow in our relationship with Him, and time to grow in our knowledge of Him. It has taken time for me to learn the lessons on my journey. God says in 2 Corinthians 12:9-10, "My grace is sufficient for you, for My strength is made perfect in weakness. Therefore, most gladly I will rather boast in my infirmities, that the power of Christ may rest upon me. Therefore, I take pleasure in infirmities in reproaches, in needs, in persecutions, in distresses, for Christ's sake. For when I am weak, then I am strong." Spend time with God and find your strength.

ω *Sapphire 6: Godly Dreams*

God says in his Word that His children are to "delight thyself also in the Lord: and he shall give thee the desires of thine heart." (Psalm 37:4) I believe that when we dream, all of heaven is dreaming for us. Without a dream, life is not fulfilled. When we dream, we trust God to take us to our heaven on earth. I dreamed many days of a happy family, a home filled with laughter, a life filled with peace. Our dream reflects our godly purpose. *If you don't dream, you don't really live.* I once heard a song and the lyrics said, "Dream big, because all of heaven is dreaming big for you." I believe God plants those dreams in our hearts, and He will make them come true. (Phil. 2:13) Dare to dream and reach for the stars.

ω *Sapphire 7: Gifts*

We are all given gifts to share. Spiritual gifts are supernatural gifts given by God for His purposes, for His service. When we are selfish with our God-given gifts, we deny our very purpose. We deny ourselves the joy of sharing those gifts. When we share our gifts, we take the focus off ourselves and put the focus on the receiver. I have been blessed with many gifts, and sharing those gifts as I have opportunity is my purpose. My purpose fills my life with meaning. "Well done good and faithful servant," are the words I want to hear when I reach heaven. Find your gift and share it with the world!

ω *Sapphire 8: Blessing*

The blessing promised is the fruit of the spirit. Galatians 5:22, "But the fruit of the Spirit is love, joy, peace, longsuffering, kindness, goodness, faithfulness, gentleness, self-control." The blessing is a life full of love, peace and joy. The blessing is to share what I have learned. The blessing is to believe without hesitation that I walked through fire for a reason.

I experienced the pain of abuse so that I can be a witness, a voice to all those paralyzed by incest. The blessing is to be a survivor and an encourager. Be a blessing!

৶৶৶

Healing and Restoration

If you or someone you know has suffered from sexual abuse, the twelve steps below, which are adapted in many recovery programs, are an introduction to the process that has been instrumental in my healing. It is not easy, and I in no way want to minimize the pain and the heartache that the incest causes. I know that the twelve-step approach is only the beginning of a journey that is life-long and arduous. View these actions as stepping-stones for day-after-day striving to expose the darkest corners of your heart's pain; this will help put you on the road to healing.

There will be struggles, days of slipping and sliding down this road, and times of despair, but there will be progress. Celebrate your victories, no matter how small! The war is won with small victories that bring you closer to the ultimate goal, complete victory in healing through the power of Jesus Christ. I know many 12-step programs speak vaguely of "your God" or of "a Higher Power." But I know Him personally; He is the Lord Jesus Christ – God in man, the Sacrifice for my sins before holy God, the One who loves me unconditionally, the One who rose from the grave – and He resides with me always through the Holy Spirit dwelling within me. He makes all the difference! History records it was a follower of Jesus who founded the twelve-step program.

Therefore, I urge you to come to know Him, and to begin today to embrace these steps:

1. Admit you were powerless over the abuse, the effects of the abuse and recognize the pain that the abuse has caused in your life. Accept that the abuse was wrong, that it hurt you deeply and it was not your fault.

2. Surrender to Jesus Christ as your Lord and Savior and believe that He can restore hope, healing and sanity. Jesus created you, loves you and never wanted you to suffer this pain. Receive His love today.

3. Make a decision to turn your will and your life over to a loving and caring Jesus Christ to walk through the darkest corners of your heart. Your surrender will depend on you forgiving God for your fate. Believe that He never wanted you to hurt, but He has a purpose for your life. Embrace the dream God has for your life.

4. Make an honest examination and fearless moral inventory of yourself, of the abuse, and its effects on your life. Find a confidant or therapist to share your deepest secrets. Purge yourself of the secrecy and of the shame. The incest was not your fault and you have nothing to be ashamed of because you did not have the power. There is more room on the outside than there is on the inside. Release the secret.

5. Confess to Jesus Christ, who desires a personal relationship with you, confess to yourself, and confess to another human being your strengths and your weaknesses. Identify your false self and begin to peel off the layers to discover your true self. Embrace your true self.

6. Be entirely ready and willing to surrender to a loving relationship with Christ Jesus to help you remove all the debilitating consequences of the abuse and become willing to treat yourself and others with respect, compassion and acceptance. Join a church home and learn to receive love. Let go of the anger and let go of the shame, embrace His love.

7. Humbly and honestly pray to Jesus Christ to remove the unhealthy and self-defeating consequences stemming from the abuse. Pray without ceasing. Pray for the strongholds of the abuse to be broken and pray for the generational sin to be broken in your life. Believe that God answers prayer. God hears you.

8. Make a list of all the people you may have harmed (of your own free will), especially yourself and your inner child, and become willing to forgive them all and ask for forgiveness. Forgiveness is a process; don't force the progress, but make a commitment and it will happen when you are emotionally ready. Forgiving from your heart is genuine and freeing. Commit to forgive out of obedience.

9. Confront those who have caused pain in your life, wherever possible, except when to do so would result in physical, mental, emotional or spiritual harm to yourself or others. Face them in a spirit of forgiveness and accept that they may not assume accountability for their actions. Be responsible for your actions, not theirs.

10. Continue to take responsibility for your own recovery and recognize patterns of behavior still dictated by the abuse. Promptly admit and alter destructive behavior. Enjoy your victories, whether large or small, and don't beat yourself up for the failures.

11. Pray and meditate on God's Word to improve your relationship with Him. Seek God's will for your life and seek God's power to carry out your mission. Open your Bible daily and God will meet you there. His Word is alive.

12. Share your spiritual awakening and healing process with others and practice these principles in all your endeavors. The more you share your testimony, the more power you will have over the abuse and the more you will identify yourself as a survivor not a victim. Sharing the secret diminishes its power. A great support group can often be a small Bible study group of Christians.

Also, consider one of the organizations listed in this Appendix under "Resource," note toll-free hotline numbers, and write the Author (angela@angelakwilliams.com).

Visit www.angelakwilliams.com to invite Angela Williams to speak at your event.

Closing Thoughts

I pray that each reader will embrace the healing power of Christ Jesus and invite Him into his or her life. A simple prayer on your knees will ensure salvation and healing.

Dear Lord, I know now that you really love me. I know also that I am a sinner, and I want to turn from my sins. I believe that you died on the cross for me. I know your blood sacrifice was the ultimate price for my sins, and I accept you now as my Lord and Savior. Please come into my heart and do a work in me and a work in my life. Take my life and use it to glorify You. I want to follow you all the days of my life. In Jesus' name, amen.

If you have prayed this prayer, and meant it in your heart, then congratulations! You have received the most precious gift in the world, and you have now embarked on your journey in salvation. Tell someone! If you are not part of a church body, pray for God to lead you to a Christ-centered place of worship. Know that churches are filled with men and women just like you with their own faults and imperfections. The church body is on a journey of growing spiritually and discovering righteousness. Don't be judgmental and don't think that anyone is judging you. Pray for a spiritual mentor who can help you mature in your walk with Christ.

The truth is a light and many people in darkness shun the light. I know God's hand has been on this book and the words written on these pages, or I wouldn't have had the strength to relive the memories, nor remember them so vividly in order to write them down. I pray the light will shine and touch those desiring to find the way through their darkness.

I also pray this book will give insight as to why I need to be loved so deeply, why I cling so tightly, why I try so hard to please and why at times there is a valve that releases anger that I cannot explain. When I felt forsaken by my biological Father, my Mother and Carl, God took me in. I now desire to be a woman after God's own heart. God didn't want me to surrender my hurts; He wanted me to surrender my heart, my broken heart, so that He could restore it. I don't want my life to be about abuse, but about restoration. He is waiting to restore you, yes you! And all who come to Him openly and honestly. He speaks in Isaiah 54:4, "Do NOT be afraid, you will not suffer shame. Do not fear disgrace: you will not be humiliated. You will forget the shame of your youth." I pray Psalms 51:12, "Restore to me again the joy of your salvation and make me willing to obey you."

God is sovereign, and it is so good to really know that. As someone has said, "When you can't trace His hand, you must trust His heart." God puts us in a position of need to do a work in us. Life change begins with an encounter with God, an encounter with the living, loving God. "The righteous cry out, the Lord hears them; he delivers them from all their troubles, the Lord is close to the brokenhearted and saves those who are crushed in spirit." (Psalm 34:18)

We can unleash the healing power of God in our lives by spending time with Him, by spending time in his Word, and by admitting our wrongs and forgiving ourselves. We each must seek balance in life – physically, mentally, emotionally and spiritually. We each must seek the true meaning of life, which is to glorify God, to worship Him in spirit and truth, to love, to laugh, especially to forgive, and to celebrate the healings He gives as we follow Him in faith, by grace.

"O my afflicted people, tempest-tossed and troubled, I will rebuild you on a foundation of sapphires."

ৡৢৡৢৡ

BIBLIOGRAPHY

• David Finkelhor, et al; *The Dark Side of Families: Current Family Violence Research*, Thousand Oaks, Ca. Sage Publications, 1985.

• "Child Abuse: America's New Plague," *Child Protection Guide*, 3rd ed. (Santa Rosa, Calif.; Christian Action Network Foundation, 1989)

• Paula Hawkins. *Children at Risk: My Fight Against Child Abuse – A Personal Story and a Public Plea*, (New York, N.Y 1986 (Adler & Adler Pub; 1st ed. Edition, September 1986)

• Darkness to Light Foundation: *Stewards of Children*. See Darkness2Light.org.

• The National Center for Victims of Crime reports: www.ncvc.org/ncvc/main.aspx?dbName=DocumentViewer&DocumentID=32360

END NOTES

[1] Source: The U.S. Department of Justice Bureau of Justice Statistics (BJS) survey of rapes reported to law enforcement agencies in 1992, [*FBI, Crime in the United States*, 1992, p. 23, 1993. June 1994, NCJ-147001].

Two Federal statistical programs provide national measures of rape incidence: the FBI's Uniform Crime Reporting (UCR) program, which records rapes reported to law enforcement agencies, and the BJS National Crime Victimization Survey (NCVS), which records reported and unreported rapes, *based on Census Bureau interviews with the American public age 12 years and older*. Neither includes data on children under the age 12! BJS 'experts' say that, "this segment of the population cannot be reliably interviewed." Children under 12 are included in the UCR Program, but UCR national statistics exclude victims with unknown ages. Consequently, neither program offers information on rape victims under 12.

[2] Darkness to Light Foundation.
   See www.darkness2light.org/7steps/step1.asp

[3] FBI: Crime in the United States 1992. In recent years, a growing number of States have adopted a more detailed reporting system in the UCR program. Data from the developing system were gathered in the BJS survey of States and used here to estimate the number of rape victims under age 12. The estimate was based on those States that indicated the number of victims under age 12 or thereabout. Data from 12 States qualified: the 5 that reported the number under 12, 4 others that reported the number age 12 and under, and 3 others that reported the number under 11. The 12 States reported ages on 23,938 victims, or 22% of the national total. Based on these data, an estimated 16% of rape victims, or 1 in 6, were under age 12. By comparison, females under 12 comprised 17% of the 1992 U.S. female population.

Applying the 16% figure from the 12 States to the national total, BJS estimated that nationwide about 17,000 girls under age 12 (16% of 109,062) were raped in 1992. This is a conservative estimate because it was derived from statistics on rapes reported to law enforcement officials and did not include unreported rapes. Also ... the 12 States that formed its basis were probably not nationally representative.

Victim-offender relationship:
   Two sources provided information on rapists: interviews with rape victims reported to law enforcement agencies in 1991 in three States (Alabama, North Dakota, and South Carolina), and 1991

293

interviews with rapists confined in the Nation's State prisons. Sources indicated similar accounts of rape victim ages: Regardless of source, when the victim was under 12, the likelihood of a family relationship was relatively high: 46% of victims and 70% of imprisoned rapists. Additional detail from the three-State survey revealed that 20% of victims under age 12, 11% of victims age 12 to 17, and 1% of those 18 or older were raped by their fathers.

[4] Paula Hawkins. *Children at Risk: My Fight Against Child Abuse – A Personal Story and a Public Plea,* Adler & Adler Pub; 1st ed. edition (September 1986)

[5] Gary L. Bauer, *Our Hopes, Our Dreams*, Chattooga Springs, (Focus on the Family Publishing, 1996), 139.

[6] David Finkelhor, et al; *The Dark Side of Families: Current Family Violence Research,* Thousand Oaks, Ca. Sage Publications, 1985.

[7] Wynonna Judd, "Testify to Love," *Touched by an Angel - The Album,* © 1998 Sony Music Entertainment Inc.

[8] Putnam, F. (2003). Ten-year update review; Child Sexual Abuse.

[9] *Journal of the American Academy of Child and Adolescent Psychiatry.* pp. 42,269-278. Cited in *Stewards of Children,* Darkness to Light Foundation, 2006, pp.12, 37.

[10] Darkness to Light Foundation. *Stewards of Children – Interactive Workbook 2000,* p. 26, et al.

[11] "*Sorrows to Sapphires*" song by *Jan Willson* available on "*It Shouldn't Hurt to be a Child*" CD. 207-777-3776. Other recovery materials available at www.hopehousemaine.com

ঙ৹ঙ৹ঙ৹

RESOURCES

The author urges you to report promptly to *someone you trust* the crimes of assault that you may be experiencing. With that trusted friend, notify authorities. Sometimes, having the courage to trust someone else is fearfully hard. That is when "hotline" telephone services can help.

However, sad to say, caution should be used by anyone approaching "help" organizations. DO NOT just web search. Credible websites are listed below. Even so, ask questions: Do any of the staff recruit to so-called alternate lifestyles? Do they advocate alternative sexual orientation? Do they believe in and offer Bible-based counseling and therapy? Do they have victorious former clients who can attest to their effectiveness? Are they licensed counselors? Do they have a list of ministerial (clergy) references?

NOTE: The author disclaims any liability or responsibility for any claims made or services provided by such organizations as are listed in this book. The following is publicly available information and is published here because these organizations have been listed by the federal government of the United States of America.

TELEPHONE HOTLINES

- VOICE Today, Inc. – www.voicetoday.org
- **National Center for Missing and Exploited Children;** 800.THE.LOST (800.843.5678); helping families and professionals (social services, law enforcement); by far the most comprehensive and official source of information.
- **HOPEHOUSE, Inc.** – Jane and Bruce Wilson: *Oil and Wine for the Wounded Study* and other healing materials at: 207.777.3776. 163 Elm Street, Mechanic Falls, ME 04256 www.hopehousemaine.com
- **National Suicide Prevention Lifeline: 1-800-s-u-i-c-i-d-e.**
- **Survivors of Incest Anonymous** World Service Office, P.O. Box 21817, Baltimore, MD 21222; 1.410.282.3400; Website: www.siawso.org. A self-help recovery program

modeled after Alcoholics Anonymous. No dues or fees. For men and women, 18 years and older, who were sexually abused as children. They specify a person will not be rejected because "you think your abuse was 'too horrible,' and you will not be discounted because you think your abuse wasn't 'bad enough to count.'"

- **Childhelp** USA National Child Abuse, 15757 N. 78th Street, Scottsdale, Arizona 85260; 1.800.4.A.CHILD (1.800.422.4453; www.childhelpusa.org. Available 24 hours a day, seven days a week. Information on where to make and file your report.
- **All States'** toll-free telephone numbers for reporting suspected child abuse, telephone the Clearinghouse at 1.800.FYI.3366.
- **National Survivors of Domestic Violence**, whose slogan is: "Break the Silence, Make the Call." 1.800.799.SAFE (7233); 1.800.787.3224 (TTY)
- **National Family Violence** 1.800.222.2000; help for family violence through taped messages.
- **Incest Awareness Foundation** Phone: 1.888.547.3222
- **Incest Hotline** 212.227. 3000; Counselors available for private, confidential conversations 24 hours a day; www.safehorizon.org
- **Incest Survivors Anonymous** 1.310.386.5599; also 1.562.428.5599 P.O. Box 17245 Long Beach, CA 90807 www.lafn.org Self-help, mutual-help recovery program for men, women, and teens. Run for and by survivors and those who helped them.
- **Child Abuse Childhelp**; 1.800.4.A.CHILD (800.422.4453); helping child-abuse victims, parents, concerned individuals.
- **Youth Crisis Hotline**; 1.800.HIT.HOME (800.448.4663); helping individuals report child abuse, youth ages 12 to 18
- **Child Sexual Abuse Stop It Now!** 1-888. PREVENT (888.773.8368); helping child sexual abuse victims, parents, offenders, concerned individuals.
- **Family Violence National Domestic Violence** 1-800.799.SAFE (800.799.7233); helping children, parents, friends, offenders.

- **Abuse Victim Hotline** (free legal advice and counsel) toll free: 877.448.8678
- **Between Friends** (800) 603.HELP (1.800.603.4357)
- **Rape, Abuse and Incest National Network:** (800) 656.4673 – (www.raain.org)
- **Child Welfare Information Gateway**: (800) 422.4453
- **Child Find of American Hotline:** (800) I.AM.LOST (800.426.5678)
- **Darkness To Light** (www.d2l.org)
- **Primary source for the above hotlines:** *U.S. Department of Health and Human Services, Administration for Children and Families; Administration on Children, Youth and Families; Children's Bureau, Child Welfare Information Gateway; Children's Bureau/ACYF; 1250 Maryland Avenue, SW; Eighth Floor; Washington, DC 20024; 703.385.7565 or 800.394.3366; Email: info@childwelfare.gov*